Survival Homestead One

Finding The Perfect Bug Out Location

Gordon Blaine

SARCO
PRESS

ISBN-13: 978-1508999065
ISBN-10: 1508999066

Table of Contents

Maps and Tables

ABOUT THIS BOOK

Survival Homestead One: Finding The Perfect Bug Out Location is the first book in a series about finding and developing a Survival Homestead or Bug Out Location. The objective of the series is to give the reader information to make the right decisions and prioritize his or her choices when mapping out such an important undertaking.

Although this book is targeted towards finding a Survival Homestead or Bug Out Location, the information here is pertinent to anyone intending to relocate to a different state.

Not all U.S. geographical areas are the same. Costs of living, gun laws, taxes and home prices can all vary wildly from state to state. This book is filled with tables and maps to give an idea the strengths and weaknesses of different parts of the country.

Most of the information in this particular volume is freely available to those who take the time to look for it, but it is scattered across the internet and searches often result in hours spent chasing dead ends, leaving a feeling of bewilderment and confusion. I located my Bug Out Location years ago and I applied my experiences and 'lessons learned' to research and compile the data and it still took me months to do. In every case I include the source of the data, and often I include more internet links so that when people narrow down an area they will know where to go to find more details.

Note: "Bug Out Location" and "Survival Homestead" don't necessarily mean the same thing. A survival homestead is always a Bug Out Location, but a Bug Out Location is not always a survival homestead. A survival homestead is a Bug Out Location developed to its ultimate potential, but the search criteria for either are similar. In addition, the information in this book has applications aside from the obvious prepper orientation. Anyone considering moving to another state will find valuable information here.

At the end of Part Three, I analyzed the data for the purpose of ranking all fifty states in order of suitability for a Bug Out Location or Survival Homestead. This was a wholly scientific study and no preconceived notions were involved in the ranking. The results are surprising.

The data I collected for the state rankings consists of the 13 categories listed below:

1. Percent of Population on Welfare
2. Avg. Annual State & Local Taxes
3. Cost of Living
4. Difference Between Monthly Avg High/Low Temperatures
5. Gun Friendliness Rank
6. Median Income
7. Population Density
8. Density of Nuclear Power Plants
9. Precipitation (inches per year)
10. Unemployment Rate (%)
11. Costs of Buying a Home
12. Violent Crime Rate
13. Potential for Solar Power Production

Each category does not add to the score with the same weight. Some categories like "Gun Friendliness" for example, have more bearing on the ranking.

Wherever possible, I include tables ranking the states in order of preference, followed by a map to give a visual aid to identify trends. Some of the maps are government issued, but most of the maps were custom made for this book. Details for the ranking methodology will be explained in a later section.

At the end of the book I have included internet links to full size maps. These can be viewed with any internet-connected device.

HOW TO USE THIS BOOK

This book is focused on how to find a suitable location for a Survival Homestead or Bug Out Location. There are twenty-one maps and fifteen statistical tables to help the reader make a decision. The tables (and most of the maps) rank the states in order of preference for the individual statistics. The statistics include climate, economy, gun laws, population density, and more.

The book is divided into the six parts listed below:

1. Why Bug Out?
2. Decide What You Need
3. Which State Is Best?
4. How to Research and Buy Real Estate
5. You Have Your Property. Now What?

If you are reading this book you are probably familiar with the concept of the Bug Out Location. In that case feel free to skip the introductory Part One (and possibly Part Two) and move directly to Part Three, where most of the information in this book is contained in the "Tables and Maps" section.

WHO IS THE AUTHOR?

And more importantly, what is it about him that makes him feel qualified to advise others on the subject of bug out locations?

What I have written here is information pulled from first hand, real world experience. In another of my books, "Montana Homestead"[1] I wrote about the circumstances that led up to my purchase of an off grid bug out property and why I chose to live there permanently. I then documented my first year and a half of life at the property and the construction of my cabin.

I don't claim to be an expert on the subject of bug out locations (and who can?) but I did spend a good amount of time researching and looking for property. Then I gained a great deal of hard experience at developing a homestead off grid in the remote woods. All on a very limited budget.

My wish is simply to pass on to others what I have learned in hope they won't make the same mistakes I made.

INTRODUCTION

It is a chilly morning in late autumn at my suburban house. I climb into my two year old Chevy to begin my daily commute to work in the city. As usual, I listen to the radio to make the forty-five minute drive a little bit less unbearable. As I stop at one of the many traffic lights on my route, the voice of Lady Gaga is interrupted by a news alert. The voices catch my attention as I irritably encourage the drivers ahead of me to hurry.

"….confirmed Iran has gained nuclear capability."

"What does this mean? Is the United States under threat?"

"The U. S. Secretary of State is currently in communication with the Iranian foreign minister…"

The conversation is lost in the background as I make the traffic light just as it turns yellow, and I forget about it. A Katy Perry song comes on the radio and I sing along, forgetting about Iran.

Flash forward a week. It is Tuesday evening and, glass of wine in hand, we are watching the latest episode of American Idol. The broadcast is interrupted by breaking news.

I'm only partially paying attention to the news broadcast (*Harry Connick, Jr. was just about to join the contestant for a duet!*), but I learn that Israel has declared war on Iran. Israeli bombers have destroyed Iranian factories and communications infrastructure. Iran has declared they will annihilate the Jews, and Pakistan and Syria have announced they will do whatever is necessary to aid their ally. Russia is mobilizing their military, and the CIA has leaked information that, according to satellite data, China is up to suspicious activity.

The broadcast cuts back to regular programming and I see that I've missed the end of American Idol.

On my way to work the next morning I stop at the gas station to fill up my Chevy and I'm amazed to see that the price of gas has more than doubled over night. At $7.99 per gallon it will cost me a hundred and fifty dollars to fill up my tank. I buy ten gallons and continue my drive to work, wondering what in the hell is going on. When I get to the office I learn that most of the Middle East is at war, and oil fields have been bombed in Iran, Iraq, and the United Arab Emirates. The price of oil is over three hundred dollars per barrel and expected to go higher.

The next week the weather is turning cold and gas is at fourteen dollars per gallon. I wonder how I will continue to buy gas to get to work. Suddenly, I realize that I haven't filled up the oil tank for the furnace.

I have begun to watch the daily news. There are lines at the filling stations and fights are breaking out. I use precious fuel to drive to the local Super Wal-Mart to stock up on groceries, but it is too late - the shelves are nearly bare. A nervous employee explains that due to the shortage of diesel fuel, fewer trucks are transporting fuel and goods.

Riots are forming in the cities and it has become dangerous to travel to populated areas. In my suburb, home invasions are becoming a common occurrence. I decide that I will not go to work the next day and I don't have enough gas to get there anyway. I will stay home with my wife and daughter. Millions of other Americans are thinking the same thing.

The railroads, which rely on diesel fuel, are still operating but it is uncertain for how long. There is no end in sight for the war in the middle east and the talking heads are saying it may continue for years. The U.S. has increased oil production but it is not enough, and most of what is produced is going to the military which has begun mobilizing for defense.

Farmers are reporting that they won't be able to plant crops in the spring because they can't get fuel for equipment or petroleum based fertilizers and pesticides. In the news broadcasts, shrill voices declare that Americans will starve in the upcoming year. They say that even if the war ended today, there has been so much damage to the middle eastern oil fields that it would take years for production to get back to normal.

Police and firefighters have stopped reporting to work - there is no fuel to transport them and many have decided to stay home to protect their families. Buildings burn out of control and in populated areas it is too dangerous to go outdoors. FEMA has set up refugee camps for the homeless and starving. The President has declared martial law and the military has begun patrolling the cities.

Just when it seems as if things can't get any worse, Islamic terrorists strike. Suicide bombers detonate at refugee camps and destroy critical electrical distribution points. We lose electric power at our house and I've heard from my neighbor that the power plant has burned down. But it didn't really matter - with the shortage of available coal for the power plant and the inability of employees to get to work, the infrastructure has begun to fail.

As I wait in line for hours at the rear of a military truck to get some MREs, I hear a rumor fly though the crowd that this is the last time the truck will stop. The crowd turns ugly and I decide to walk home without my food and water.

For weeks we've hunkered down in our house in the suburb. I try to remember how long it's been since my life turned upside down. It feels like it has been years. My wife is exhausted and my little girl is sobbing. There is no food left in the house. My throat is tight and swollen with helplessness as I realize that my daughter will starve to death.

I hear gunshots from the neighbor's house and I think about going over to see what's going on. But my wife begs me to stay. There is no way to call 911 and it wouldn't help if I could - they hadn't answered the phone in the last days while the cell service was still working.

I lock the doors and take the wife and daughter into the bathroom and cover us with a thick blanket to try to stay warm. I wish we had left the suburb weeks ago, but I had convinced myself that the crisis would fizzle out and things would return to normal. The truth was that I had no plan and nowhere to go.

Anything would be better than being here in this house in the suburbs, I think. In the darkness, I squeeze my wife's shoulder to reassure her and I can sense that she is desperate. For the first time in my life, I wish I had a gun.

The neighborhood is quiet. I imagine that the intruders have murdered Mike and Elly and are now searching their house for food. I understand that nothing matters except getting something to eat because we haven't eaten in days. I know it's only a matter of time.

I close my eyes. In the back of my mind, I wonder how long until the intruders come for us.

Prepping and Bugging Out

The preceding story was not science fiction. There are no zombies or alien invaders. Yet for that family, the end of the world has come. If the main character had paid attention and been prepared, he might have been able to keep his family safe. We can't depend on the government to keep us safe; it is up to us.

Contrary to the way "preppers" are portrayed on television, preppers are not all eccentric paranoids. There are real reasons to prepare. A shortage of fuel, or a breakdown of the electrical infrastructure will limit the ability of trucks to transport goods. Grocery stores only have the food in stock that is on their shelves. They don't have more food in a storeroom in the back. If the store doesn't get resupplied within days, the shelves will become bare. People will starve.

Natural disasters and war are just a couple things to prepare for. Stockpiling food and water, and keeping firearms and ammunition (and training with those firearms) is a way to prepare for these kinds of events.

But if the situation degrades to the point where we are no longer safe in our homes, it is time to leave for a more secure location. The time has come to "bug out".

But to where do we bug out? Some people have a vague idea they will simply travel to a less populated area. Some will put on a backpack and head for the woods. Others will drive to the house of a friend or relative.

Some of us will go to our bug out location. Ideally, the bug out location will be stockpiled with food and water. The best Bug Out Location will have the potential to provide food and water indefinitely because it is not inconceivable that the event which caused us to bug out will change our ways of life for years.

This book is for those of us wishing to search for and buy an ideal Bug Out Location. The bulk of the book is aimed at providing information about geographical areas within the continental United States.

The Bug Out Location should be located in an area that will enable us to thrive if we need to evacuate to it, but we may never need to use our Bug Out Location for its intended purpose. We need to consider things such as taxes and the gun laws in the state. In other words, we need to view it as if we are buying property for a retirement home or a recreational property. For that reason I have included information such as the tax rates and gun friendliness of each area.

Part One:

Why Bug Out?

WHAT IS A BUG OUT LOCATION?

In the introduction, war has broken out in the Middle East and the protagonist is stuck in his suburban house while fires burn and neighbors' houses are invaded by thugs. It would be better if there was a safe place to go far from the violence and starving masses to wait out the crisis until the situation normalized.

The purpose of a Bug Out Location is to provide food, water, shelter and safety in the case of a temporary or permanent crisis requiring abandonment of the normal home.

A Bug Out Location might be safe place to hang out for a few days while things get back to normal or it may be where we go to start a new life when the world as we know it ends. It might be a friends house in the country or a hardened bunker. Perhaps a secret cave in the woods or an abandoned factory. It can be a single-family cabin or a massive compound that can house a group of families. In the most desperate circumstances there may be no distinguishing feature at all to a Bug Out Location - it might be a secluded field in which to pitch a tent. Food and water can be stored permanently at the Bug Out Location or brought to the location at the time of crisis. The Bug Out Location may or may not have a shelter. The point I'm getting at is that the definition of a Bug Out Location is wholly subjective to the user.:

- Secluded camping spot
- Abandoned building
- Rural farmhouse belonging to family or friends
- Weekend cabin in the woods
- Full time homestead

A short term or long term crisis might necessitate the relocation of a person or family to a Bug Out Location. A short term crises may be a natural disaster such as a forest fire or hurricane. Longer term crises may include job loss, total economic meltdown, or a massive burst of solar wind and magnetic fields being released into space and destroying earths communications and electrical infrastructure in the form of a coronal mass ejection[2].

Survival Homestead

A Survival Homestead meets the criteria of a Bug Out Location, but it is occupied full time. A Survival Homestead is a Bug Out Location taken to the next level. If we live on our Survival Homestead, raise our own food, and are prepared so that if the world collapses around us and we hardly notice, we have achieved the end-goal of survivalists: the Survival Homestead.

To Bug Out or Hunker Down

The argument can be made that it is better to hunker down at home and ride out the crisis.

Depending on the location and the crisis, its likely true. If your residence is distantly located from a major city in rural farming country, I'd recommend staying put. (But those aren't the people reading this book!)

On the other hand, I remember hurricane Katrina. Katrina was a short term crisis, but staying put was not an option. Natural disasters can make us realize that a Bug Out Location can be helpful in even the most mundane situations.

Lawlessness and riots can form in the larger cities even in a short term crisis. During the Rodney King riots in L.A there was violence for weeks and the thugs were looting, starting fires and shooting at the firemen who arrived. I would not have enjoyed being a resident of the area at the time.

When to Bug Out?

When a local or worldwide crisis develops, how do we know when it is time to abandon home (and possibly our career) and head to the Bug Out Location?

Will automobile traffic slow or halt your escape? If you live in a metro area you might need to get out of dodge before the rest of the city gets the same idea. You may need to leave days before the rest of the population comes to the same conclusion.

If we live in a rural area and the Bug Out Location is relatively close to home we can go at any time. We might have to drive a little further to work the next morning if it turns out to be nothing, but the peace of mind in knowing that our family and possessions are safe will help to ease that burden.

If the Bug Out Location is hundreds of miles away from the home things become complicated. You must make sure you have enough fuel to get there - gas may not be available on the way. Roads may be closed or otherwise unusable. Thieves and murderers may lie in wait to take what you have.

The only thing we can do is pay close attention to the news and always make sure we have fuel and multiple routes to get to where we need to go.

Part Two:

Decide What You Need

What Are The Requirements?

The geographic location of the Bug Out Location will have the most effect on the survivability of the inhabitants. The location will determine the climate (and seasonal temperature) and the likelihood of discovery by strangers.

I searched for land for months in the papers and on internet real estate web sites before buying my Bug Out Location. I walked dozens of properties. It took a long time to find what I needed.

Our potential property had to meet certain criteria. I printed a list of these and gave it to our local real estate agent:

1. Source of water: drilled well, surface water (pond, creek, stream), spring, rainfall catchment.
2. Woodlot for firewood and building materials
3. Southern exposure for gardening and solar power
4. Some level terrain for structures: dwellings and outbuildings
5. Some land to grow food: reasonably flat or terraced
6. Climate which will allow growing food
7. If no grid utilities, must have cell phone reception
8. Year round access, even if a four wheel drive vehicle may be required
9. Full water, mineral and timber rights
10. At least 5 acres
11. Seclusion
12. No restrictions or covenants
13. No Home Owner's Association
14. Limited building codes
15. Potential for a septic system (but there are ways around this)

Other factors include annual rainfall, taxes, political climate, population density and availability of electricity.

In addition, we have some personal requirements. We may desire a milder climate because that's what we like, or we may need the location to be relatively close to hospitals or good schools or a form of employment. Sometimes we simply want a pretty view.

Long Term or Short Term?

Will the Bug Out Location be a solution for the short term or long term? In other words, are we planning to hide out for a few months while the economic meltdown dissipates or do we want to ride out the zombie apocalypse?

A short term Bug Out Location is a simple place to keep your head down for a few months. Food, water and other supplies can be stored at the Bug Out Location or brought in at the time of crisis.

A long term Bug Out Location will need a more comfortable shelter, a local source of water and, depending on the anticipated length of stay, a larger store of food or a way to produce it.

At the far end of the spectrum is the Bugout Homestead where the users live full time. When we get to this point we can say that we have already "bugged out" and we are living in our Bug Out Location.

Should We Live Permanently At The Bug Out Location?

Before we start looking for the Bug Out Location we need to decide if we are going to use it as a back up location or live there full time. There are pros and cons with both ideas.

Live Away From Bug Out Location

There are advantages if the Bug Out Location is not our primary residence. The Bug Out Location can be more remote, have smaller living quarters, be of a smaller acreage, and have a more primitive electrical and plumbing infrastructure. We can spend less money on our Bug Out Location and put our money into our permanent home.

A part time Bug Out Location can serve other purposes. It might be a vacation cabin in the woods or a place to go hunting. If security is not a concern we can store our extra junk at the Bug Out Location and keep it out of site of the neighbors. If a friend or relative needs a place to stay for awhile a Bug Out Location might be perfect for that, although you should limit the number of people who know about your Bug Out Location to those who you can trust.

Live At the Bug Out Location

Most who have a Bug Out Location do not live there permanently. Most of the reasons have to do the lower population density and lack of a nearby metro area. This causes a few issues and I'll list the main ones below:

1. Fewer well paying jobs means less potential income
2. Fewer good schools for the kids
3. Increased distance from good hospitals
4. Increased distance from shopping centers and building materials
5. Lack of restaurants, cultural activities and arts entertainment
6. Increased distance from emergency services
7. Difficulty accessing the property if remote
8. Isolation

Not everyone will agree that everything on the list is a drawback and in fact these are what make the place a good Bug Out Location in the to begin with!

Some of the benefits of living at the Bug Out Location full time:

1. If a crisis happens, you are already at your Bug Out Location with all your belongings
2. The Bug Out Location may be established with water and food production - a garden, livestock and food forest
3. Less worry about theft and vandalism at an unoccupied property
4. Better relationships developed with the local community and neighbors
5. If the Bug Out Location is off grid, no adjustment needs to be made to survive without electricity

To live full time in a Bug Out Location will mark the beginning of the change into a Survival Homestead. But it requires a large commitment and possibly a drastic change in lifestyle. Unless we can make a good income working from home or spend hours commuting to work, we must live a frugal life. This can be mitigated if we have a retirement income, but on the other hand, the cost of living may be lower so the retiree might be better off than living in the city.

Grid Tied or Off Grid?

One of the most important considerations to make when buying property is, does it make a difference if the land is "off grid" or "on grid"?

In the context of this book, "off grid" means "not connected to the electrical grid". Specifically, no physical infrastructure exists to connect to the electrical grid. The lack of physical infrastructure can be due to a few reasons but a likely reason would be that the property is remotely located.

Grid-tied properties have the advantage of relatively reliable electrical power. Starting a bugout location that has grid power can be a huge advantage during the building and living process. We use grid power to do more than we realize - for example a country home with a well pump uses grid power every time someone takes a shower.

Off grid properties are more likely to be remote and that means secluded and hidden from the starving masses from the cities who scour the countryside in search of food.

In addition, secluded off grid properties have potential wild game hunting. We may not be hunters now, but who can say what will happen when the SHTF?

The most notable difference between on grid and off grid properties is usually the purchase price. Grid tied properties are often much more expensive than an identical off grid property. The reason may be as simple as the fact that grid tied properties are more often located nearer a city and comes with the resulting inflated real estate prices. My own bugout property is located off grid. Early in my search for property, I realized that grid tied properties were beyond my budget and focused on remote off grid hunting properties.

I will mention another possible advantage of an off grid location, especially if you spend considerable pre-SHTF time there. Living or spending time off grid enables you to cut the leash. You will become accustomed to an off grid lifestyle.

If the SHTF and you plan to spend your bugout time without electricity, it is best to adjust your lifestyle now when you have a relatively stress-free time in which to do it. This is when you find out how much lamp oil you really need or when you figure out how you will keep the venison cold. The best way to do this is to actually live that way for awhile.

Maybe you *do* plan to live with some form of electrical power when the SHTF. You will learn how to conserve electricity, get first hand experience at how to generate it via solar, wind, or hydro power, and constantly think about how to do things without needing electricity to save your battery banks.

What is it like to live off grid?

Living with grid electricity allows us to take things for granted. If we need a light; we flip a switch. Want to leave the television on all day? No big deal. Need to fire up the air compressor or welder? Nothing to it.

Off grid living is different. I watch every watt and I keep track of the sun to see if we are getting solar charging. I maintain our batteries. I use gasoline to run the generator.

Buying and installing a solar power system seems like an easy way to cut ties with the grid and increase our independence. But there are two things to consider; solar power is expensive, and living off grid can be difficult. Not everyone can do it.

But if we design things correctly, we can have indoor plumbing and televisions and most things that other folks have. We just have to be a little more careful about shutting of the things we aren't using.

In my opinion, the sense of independence is well worth the sacrifice.

Security

We are mainly concerned with two types of security: the security of the Bug Out Location while it is unattended and your personal security and security of property while staying at the Bug Out Location during or after the crisis.

Unattended Bug Out Location

If your Bug Out Location is in a remote area it will be subject to vandalism and theft if left unattended. My own Bug Out Location is somewhat remote and located deep in the forests of Montana but in these contemporary times with the abundance of meth addicts, it seems that nowhere is safe. If your secluded Bug Out Location appears mostly uninhabited, thieves *will* eventually find it and raid it for things they can sell to support their habit. It is disheartening but something we must deal with.

This threat can be mitigated somewhat by the presence of neighbors, but only if a working relationship has been developed. I was fortunate in that I developed a good relationship with the neighbor down the road, who volunteered to occasionally ride over on his ATV and check on my tools and equipment. I had kept most of the tools in a 20 foot steel shipping container secured with a heavy padlock, but any padlock can be disable with determination. And meth heads can be determined.

After a shelter has been constructed the threat of vandalism and thievery is compounded. My shipping container was difficult to break into and there was no way to see what was inside, offering less enticement to potential thieves. But a residential structure, no matter how primitive, hints at loot inside to be taken.

The best way to prevent theft is to occupy the Bug Out Location full time. The second best way is to make sure the thieves never find the shelter or any structures while it is left unattended. The only practical way to do this would be to make the structure almost completely underground and camouflage the entrances. This will be discussed more in the chapter on shelters.

Frequent visits to the Bug Out Location will lessen the chances of theft or vandalism. Thieves search for easy targets and properties that seem to be occupied are more likely to be avoided. Maintaining the property, outdoor motion lights and indoor lighting on timers can also help. Leaving a vehicle parked at the site may help make the property seem occupied. I've heard of motion activated alarms that will trigger the sound of a big dog barking inside the house. Combined with large "Beware of Dog!" signs, it might make a difference.

Cash, food and equipment can be buried in caches at the Bug Out Location. This is also an option if you live at the Bug Out Location full time either before or during a crisis. If your Bug Out Location is ransacked you will have a backup that you can retrieve.

Whether or not there is a structure on the property, cameras can be installed to maintain surveillance. This will not prevent the loss of property but may aid in the apprehension of the thieves and to prevent repeat thefts by the same individuals. Simple game cameras can be placed in strategic places but they must be hidden or observant thieves will see them and remove the photographic evidence.

An alternative to game cameras is IP cameras which are available for less than $100. Unlike game cameras, IP cameras transmit video across the internet, where they can be observed from a remote location. They can trigger an alarm if movement is detected to notify the owner. If thieves or vandals are observed in real time on the IP camera the sheriff's department may be called in order to have the trespassers arrested. The possible drawback of inviting law enforcement onto the property but the circumstances would surely compensate.

IP cameras need a connection to the internet. In a remote off grid Bug Out Location property the simplest way to provide the internet connection is to use a cellular wi-fi hot spot available from most cellular carries for a monthly fee. If one is skilled with electronics an old cell phone can be hacked to provide the connection, but the monthly fee still applies.

Both the cameras and the hot spot will need a power supply, which can complicate things if the Bug Out Location is off grid. In an ideal setup, the cameras and the hot spot will both be operated from a direct connection to a 12 volt DC heavy duty battery which in turn is charged by a small solar panel (these must be hidden carefully!) so it would pay to know the power requirements of the equipment (in terms of the input voltage and the power used in amps or watts) before purchasing. If the equipment must be powered via an AC adapter a small inverter can be added to the battery circuit. This adds complexity but may be easier for some users.

Attended Bug Out Location

If a world-changing event has forced one to evacuate to the Bug Out Location, security will be the number one priority. This book is concerned with finding and preparing a Bug Out Location before the crisis, but I will touch on a few things about post-apocalypse security strategies.

A Bug Out Location *can* be defended against a small group of unorganized rogues, if thought and preparation are performed ahead of time. A group like this might move on to easier pickings if the challenge is great enough.

The shelter can be built to withstand some small arms fire. Underground or masonry structures would be ideal. The building should also be resistant to fire.

The position of the shelter and the terrain of the Bug Out Location can be prepared ahead of time with defense in mind. The surrounding area should be cleared of vegetation to prevent bad guys from using it as cover or concealment.

One of the most important elements of any battle is intelligence. It is better to know the enemy is coming before they knock on the door, and to know their strengths and weaknesses.

If the population of the Bug Out Location or the surrounding community is large enough, roving patrols can be maintained to identify threats and possibly take action.

Direct communication with the surrounding community is critical. Perhaps a neighbor has a house overlooking the road in. If he observes visitors he can communicate to the rest of the neighbors over short range CB radio. Trees can be dropped in roads, defenders can take to the woods with scoped rifles, and children can be relocated to a stronger position.

But if it gets to that point things have become desperate. If your Bug Out Location is sufficiently hidden and a good distance from any well traveled roads it may never be discovered. In my opinion this is the *most important consideration* of a Bug Out Location because I think nothing is secure against a prolonged, organized assault. If the intruders are determined and equipped, they will either destroy the shelter or get inside. If a military group is performing the assault you might as well surrender or plan on taking out as many as you can before you die.

Part Three:

Which State Is Best?

Criteria

The bulk of this book is concerned with choosing in which US state to find Bug Out Location property. The book contains ranking tables and maps to help the user narrow down the choices, which may seem overwhelming.

I've used many criteria when ranking the states, and have included other criteria for consideration even if they don't factor into the rankings:

Climate:
Suitability for growing plants
Consideration for heating and cooling
Drought tendency
Renewable energy potential: solar, wind & biomass
Economy:
Taxes
Cost of living
Income potential
Poverty & Welfare
Unemployment Rate
Cost of Buying a Home
Gun laws
Crime
Population density
Proximity to nuclear power plants

Some of the states are relatively large and have many sub-regions that should be considered. For example, eastern Montana differs greatly from western Montana in terms of climate. It is recommended that once a state has been chosen, more research should be conducted at the county level. The web links in the footnotes section can provide more detailed information for the reader.

However, many of the state-by-state criteria used in this book will affect the entire state. For example, taxes and gun laws are similar throughout the state.

Maps are provided in order to enable the reader to get an idea of how the states rank at a glance. Tables are provided for more detailed statistics.

Climate

While choosing a state in which to locate a Bug Out Location or Survival Homestead, the local climate may be the most important consideration for some preppers.

The climate-related data included in this book are:

1. USDA Plant Hardiness Zones
2. Heating and Cooling Degree Days
3. Drought tendency
4. Renewable energy potential in the form of solar power and wind power

The above data does not affect the ranking of the states at the end of the book, but are included as more detailed information for the reader.

Additional climate related data used for ranking the states include:

1. Difference Between Monthly Avg High/Low Temperatures
2. Yearly Avg. Hours of Solar Potential
3. Average Annual Precipitation

Plant Hardiness Zones

The ultimate Bug Out Location should be located in an area

where it is possible to grow food in order to survive long-term. There are tools to help us choose the best location, and to help us to choose plants that will grow in those locations..

In order to help gardeners determine which plants are likely to survive in their location, the USDA developed a set of maps divided into "zones". Zones are arranged according to the average annual minimum temperature of the area.

Most seed packets and starter plants, including trees and bushes, have gardening zone information printed on the packet or on a tag. The gardening zone associated with the plant is sometimes defined as a range; for example Zone 3A - 8A. This would mean that the plant should survive in any of the zones in that range.

For example we can find that lemon trees survive in garden zones 8, 9, and 10. Looking at the map, we can see that lemon trees won't survive in the northern areas of the United States.

On the following pages are a table explaining the temperatures relative to the gardening zones and the USDA gardening zone map[3] for the continental United States. This map will give a broad idea of the zones. When determining the gardening zone for a specific location it is preferable to visit the USDA web site and use the interactive map, where zone information will be more precise. One way to operate the interactive map is to enter the zip code of a location into the text box, but one can also view individual state maps and zoom in to highly detailed levels.

It should be noted that although most of Alaska suffers from frigid cold during the winter, the extreme south-coastal areas (the "Maritime" section of Alaska) have hardiness zones of 6 or even higher! However, all of the inland portions of the state range from 2A to 4A; suitable for short season crops only. The population density of most of Alaska is around two people per square mile and there is real estate for sale in the Maritime area. So Alaska may end up being a top contender for the best state for a survival homestead.

Hardiness zone information does not affect the ranking of the states, and the maps supplied here are provided as more information for the reader.

To view full size maps,tables and links to other related information at the author's web site:

<https://gordonblaine.wordpress.com/>

Map: USDA Plant Hardiness Zones

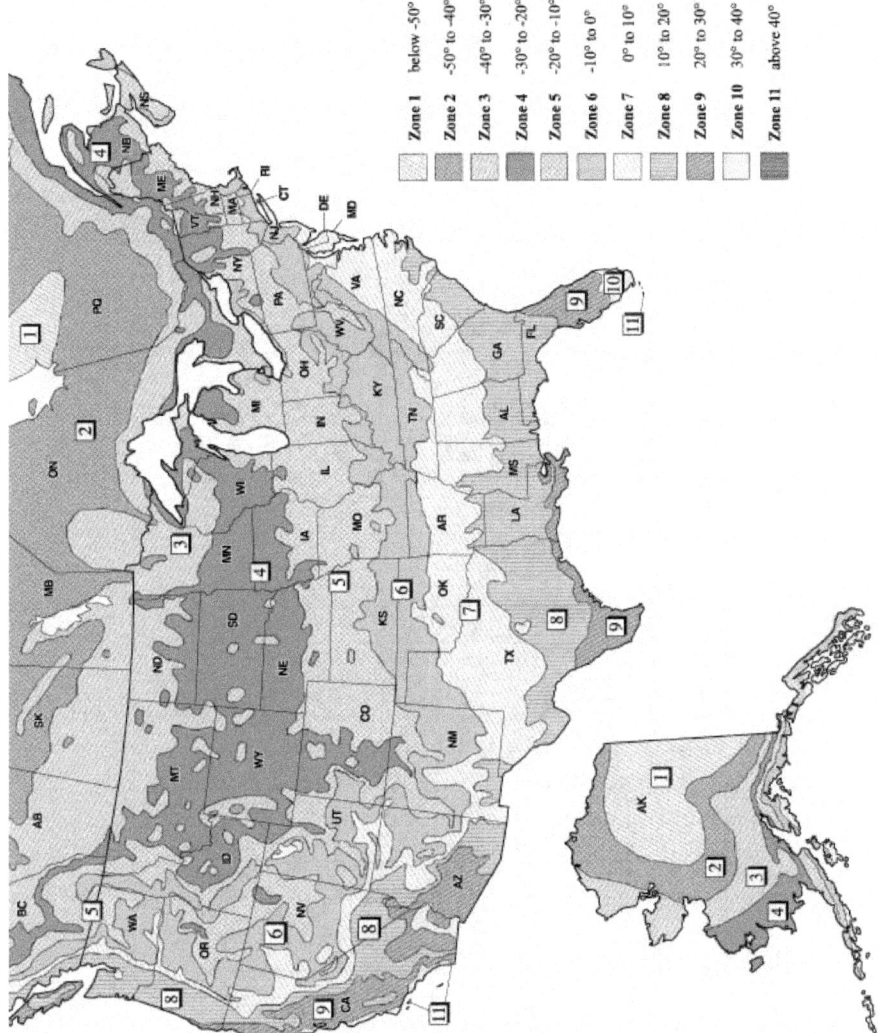

Source: U.S. Department of Agriculture[3]
For an interactive, color map with more detailed information, visit the
USDA's Plant Hardiness Zone Map web site at
http://www.planthardiness.ars.usda.gov.

Table: USDA Plant Hardiness Zone Temperatures

Zone		From	To
0	a	< −53.9 °C (−65 °F)	
	b	−53.9 °C (−65 °F)	−51.1 °C (−60 °F)
1	a	−51.1 °C (−60 °F)	−48.3 °C (−55 °F)
	b	−48.3 °C (−55 °F)	−45.6 °C (−50 °F)
2	a	−45.6 °C (−50 °F)	−42.8 °C (−45 °F)
	b	−42.8 °C (−45 °F)	−40 °C (−40 °F)
3	a	−40 °C (−40 °F)	−37.2 °C (−35 °F)
	b	−37.2 °C (−35 °F)	−34.4 °C (−30 °F)
4	a	−34.4 °C (−30 °F)	−31.7 °C (−25 °F)
	b	−31.7 °C (−25 °F)	−28.9 °C (−20 °F)
5	a	−28.9 °C (−20 °F)	−26.1 °C (−15 °F)
	b	−26.1 °C (−15 °F)	−23.3 °C (−10 °F)
6	a	−23.3 °C (−10 °F)	−20.6 °C (−5 °F)
	b	−20.6 °C (−5 °F)	−17.8 °C (0 °F)
7	a	−17.8 °C (0 °F)	−15 °C (5 °F)
	b	−15 °C (5 °F)	−12.2 °C (10 °F)
8	a	−12.2 °C (10 °F)	−9.4 °C (15 °F)
	b	−9.4 °C (15 °F)	−6.7 °C (20 °F)
9	a	−6.7 °C (20 °F)	−3.9 °C (25 °F)
	b	−3.9 °C (25 °F)	−1.1 °C (30 °F)
10	a	−1.1 °C (30 °F)	+1.7 °C (35 °F)
	b	+1.7 °C (35 °F)	+4.4 °C (40 °F)
11	a	+4.4 °C (40 °F)	+7.2 °C (45 °F)
	b	+7.2 °C (45 °F)	+10 °C (50 °F)
12	a	+10 °C (50 °F)	+12.8 °C (55 °F)
	b	> +12.8 °C (55 °F)	

Source: U.S. Department of Agriculture[3]

Temperature

Some people may be intolerant of heat and others may be intolerant of cold. But aside from those situations there are advantages and disadvantages to either.

Do the temperatures at the location have an impact on the long-term survivability of the Bug Out Location? Colder locations tend to have shorter growing seasons and to require heating fuel. Warmer locations tend to have higher population density and more insects, including termites. In either case an argument can be made that one is better than the other and except in extreme cases, the decision may be entirely a personal choice.

But I do believe that all other things being equal, a state with a mild temperature will have the edge on a state with extreme temperatures, so consideration is given in the ranking tables. Using data from the National Climatic Data Center[4], I ranked the states in order of the least amount of departure from the national annual average median temperature (51.2°F).

Table: States Ranked By Departure From Median Temperature

Rank	State	Difference From Median Average temperature	Score	Rank	State	Difference From Median Average temperature	Score
1	Indiana	0.5	100	26	Tennessee	6.4	50
1	Ohio	0.5	100	27	Idaho	6.8	48
3	Illinois	0.6	96	27	Michigan	6.8	48
3	West Virginia	0.6	96	29	New Hampshire	7.4	44
5	Rhode Island	1.1	92	30	North Carolina	7.8	42
6	Nevada	1.3	90	31	Wisconsin	8.1	40
7	New Jersey	1.5	88	32	California	8.2	38
8	Connecticut	2.2	86	33	Vermont	8.3	36
8	New Mexico	2.2	86	34	Oklahoma	8.4	34
10	Nebraska	2.4	82	35	Montana	8.5	32
10	Pennsylvania	2.4	82	36	Arizona	9.1	30
12	Utah	2.6	78	37	Arkansas	9.2	28
13	Oregon	2.8	76	37	Wyoming	9.2	28
14	Washington	2.9	74	39	Minnesota	10	24
15	Maryland	3	72	40	Maine	10.2	22
16	Kansas	3.1	70	41	North Dakota	10.8	20
17	Massachusetts	3.3	68	42	South Carolina	11.2	18
17	Missouri	3.3	68	43	Alabama	11.6	16
19	Iowa	3.4	64	44	Mississippi	12.2	14
20	Virginia	3.9	62	45	Georgia	12.3	12
21	Delaware	4.1	60	46	Texas	13.6	10
22	Kentucky	4.4	58	47	Louisiana	15.2	8
23	New York	5.8	56	48	Hawaii	18.8	6
24	South Dakota	6	54	49	Florida	19.5	4
25	Colorado	6.1	52	50	Alaska	24.6	2

Source: National Climatic Data Center[4]

Map: States Ranked By Departure From Median Temperature

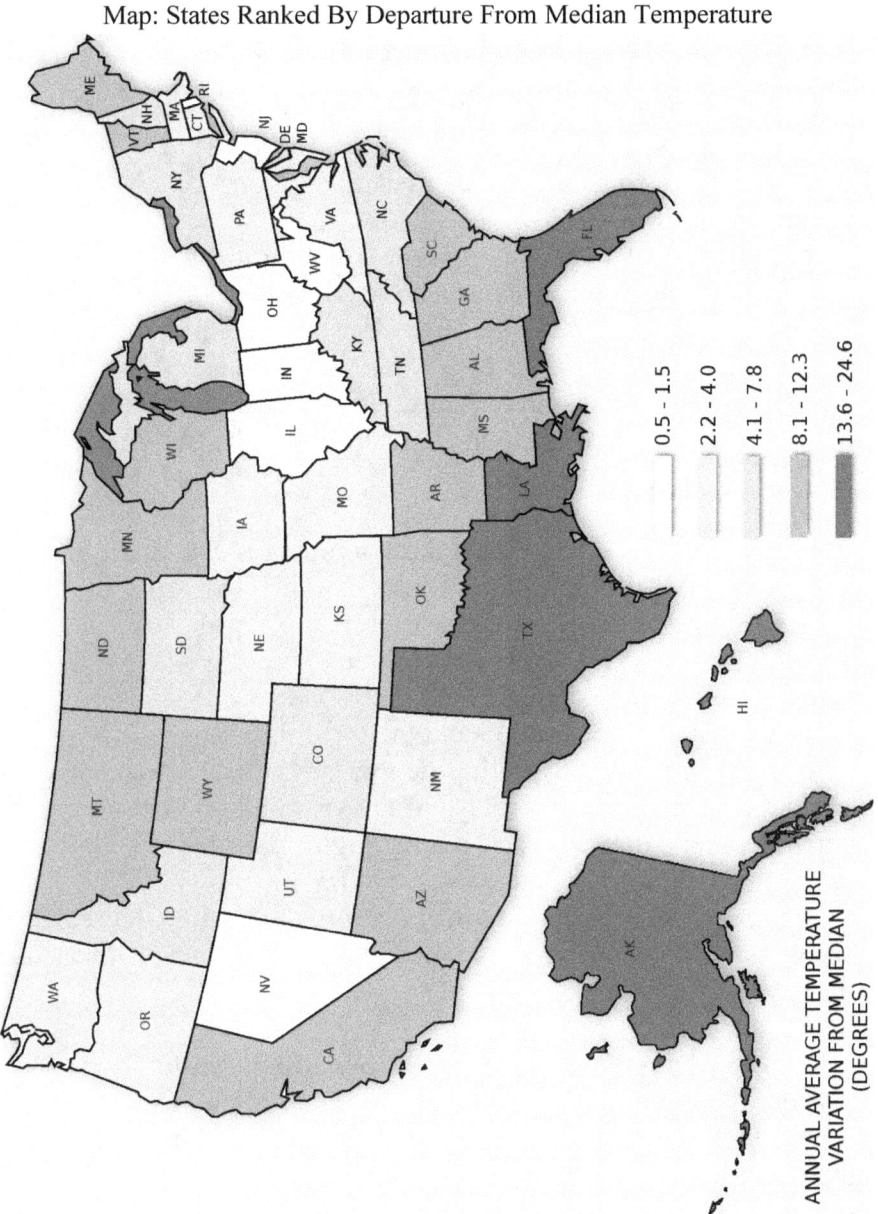

0.5 - 1.5
2.2 - 4.0
4.1 - 7.8
8.1 - 12.3
13.6 - 24.6

ANNUAL AVERAGE TEMPERATURE
VARIATION FROM MEDIAN
(DEGREES)

Source: National Climatic Data Center[4]

Heating and Cooling Degree Days

An area's "degree days" can be a factor in determining how much energy will be required to heat (or cool) the Bug Out Location. The concept of degree days can be difficult to understand yet it is worthwhile to know.

The purpose of degree days is to provide a universal way to estimate how much energy must be used to heat or cool a home. The two important types of degree days are heating degree days and cooling degree days.

Heating degree days are a measurement of how much (and for how many days) the outside air temperature is below the baseline of 65°F. (Note: all temperatures in this book are in degrees Fahrenheit.)

On a given day, add the highest temperature and the lowest temperature and divide the result by 2. This will give the days average temperature. For example, if on April 3rd, the low temperature was 55°F and the high temperature was 70°F, the average temperature is 62.5°F.

Then subtract 62.5 from 65 and the result is 2.5.

So April 3rd has 2.5 heating degree days. Add up the heating degree days for all the other days of the year and you have the total annual heating degree days. (Cooling degree days are calculated by *adding* the daily average temperature to 65!)

Combined with some other information, the heating degree days can allow us to estimate how wood we need to burn to heat our house.

Using Heating Degree Days Information

There are complex formulas to determine exact energy requirements for heating a home and they involve heating degree days, heat loss of the house, solar gain, and other factors. But I'm going to keep things simple and use rough estimates.

We'll estimate the heating of a 1,200 square foot Bug Out cabin in Bismarck, North Dakota.

First, I'll go to the Degree Days website (see text below) to find the heating degree days for the previous year. In the "Weather station ID" text box I'll enter "Bismarck, ND" and click the

"Station Search" button. A list of weather stations will be presented. I chose the "KNDBISMA2: Rural North Bismarck" station for this example.

Making sure "Heating", "Fahrenheit", and "65°F" are selected and the period covered is "Last 12 months", I click "Generate Degree Days" and gave the web site a minute to crunch numbers. Then I clicked the "Download Now" button at the top of the web page to download a text file similar to this:

Month starting,HDD
2014-01-01,1666
2014-02-01,1621
2014-03-01,1248
2014-04-01,772
2014-05-01,384
2014-06-01,152
2014-07-01,80
2014-08-01,76
2014-09-01,279
2014-10-01,574
2014-11-01,1339
2014-12-01,1413

I added the heating degree days for all the months to get 9,604 degree days. So our home in Bismarck, North Dakota is in an area with 9,604 annual heating degree days.

Using a simple formula we can get a rough estimate of how many BTUs it will take to heat our 1,200 square foot cabin. A certain number of BTUs are required to heat each square foot of cabin. We multiply the heating degree days by the square footage of the cabin, then by a factor ranging from 6 to 12. If the cabin is super insulated, use 6 BTUs per square foot. If the cabin is poorly insulated, use 12 BTUs per square foot:

Insulation Level	BTUs per sq ft
Good	6
Average	8
Fair	10
Poor	12

For this exercise, we'll use 10 BTUs per square foot, which is close to the insulation level of modern homes:

9,604 HDD x 1,200 sq ft x 10 BTU's/sq ft = 115,248,000 BTUs

So 115.25 million BTUs will be required to heat our 1,200 sq ft house for one year. One cord of Douglas Fir provides 20.7 million BTUs of heat. We can estimate that about five and a half cords of Douglas Fir firewood will be required to heat the house for one year.

This is a rough estimate and the actual heat required to heat a house depends on many factors. In addition, the number of Heating Degree Days changes every year. It may be a good idea to get a few years worth of data before doing the math.

For More Information

Detailed and updated or historical degree day statistics can be found at the National Weather Service web site[5]. The National Climatic Data Center[4] has other useful information including an interactive map to find specific targeted climate information. Another online source for[7] easy to use degree day related data is Degree Days[6]. The source of their data is The Weather Underground[7].

To get more more information about how many BTUs are required to heat a home, try one of the online BTU calculators, such as the one at www.calculators.net[8].

On the following pages are maps with the heating degree days and cooling degree days for the United States.

Degree day information does not affect the ranking of the states, and the maps supplied here are provided as more information for the reader.

Map: Heating Degree Days

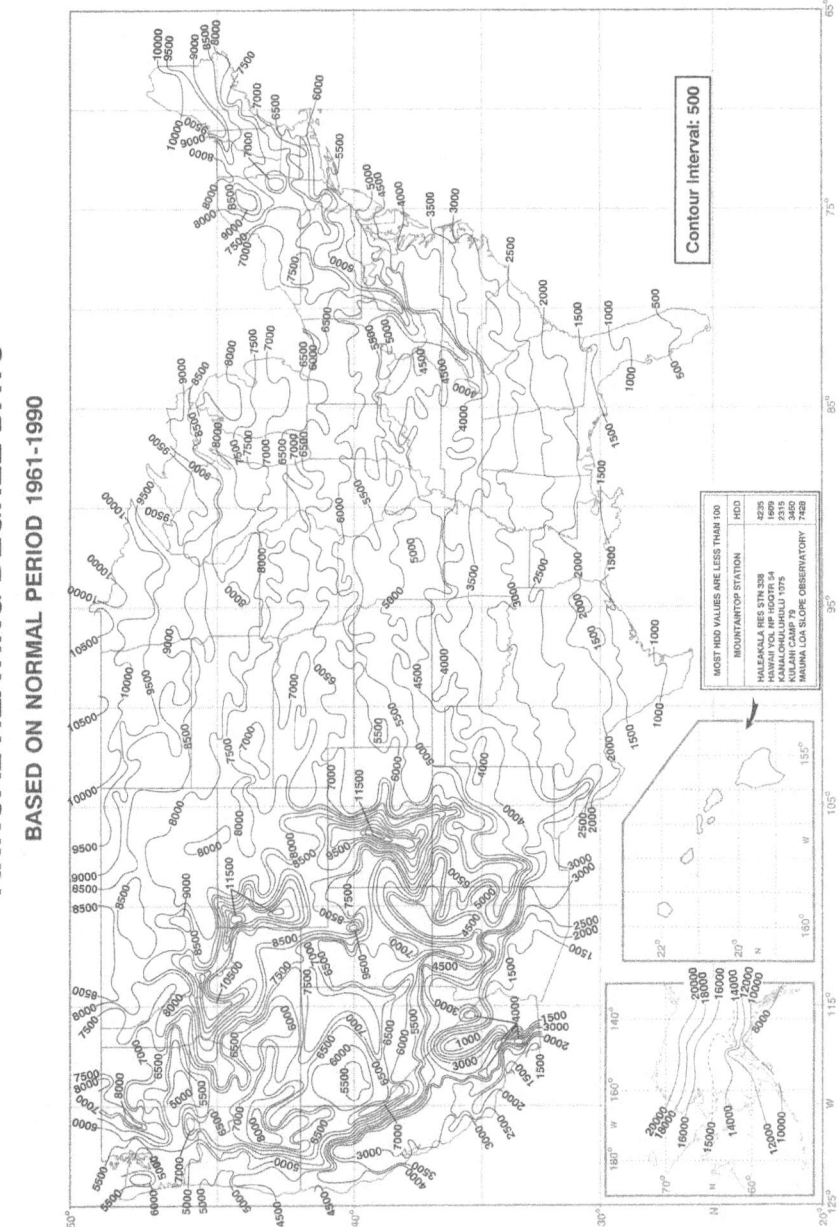

Source: National Climatic Data Center[9]

GORDON BLAINE

Map: Cooling Degree Days

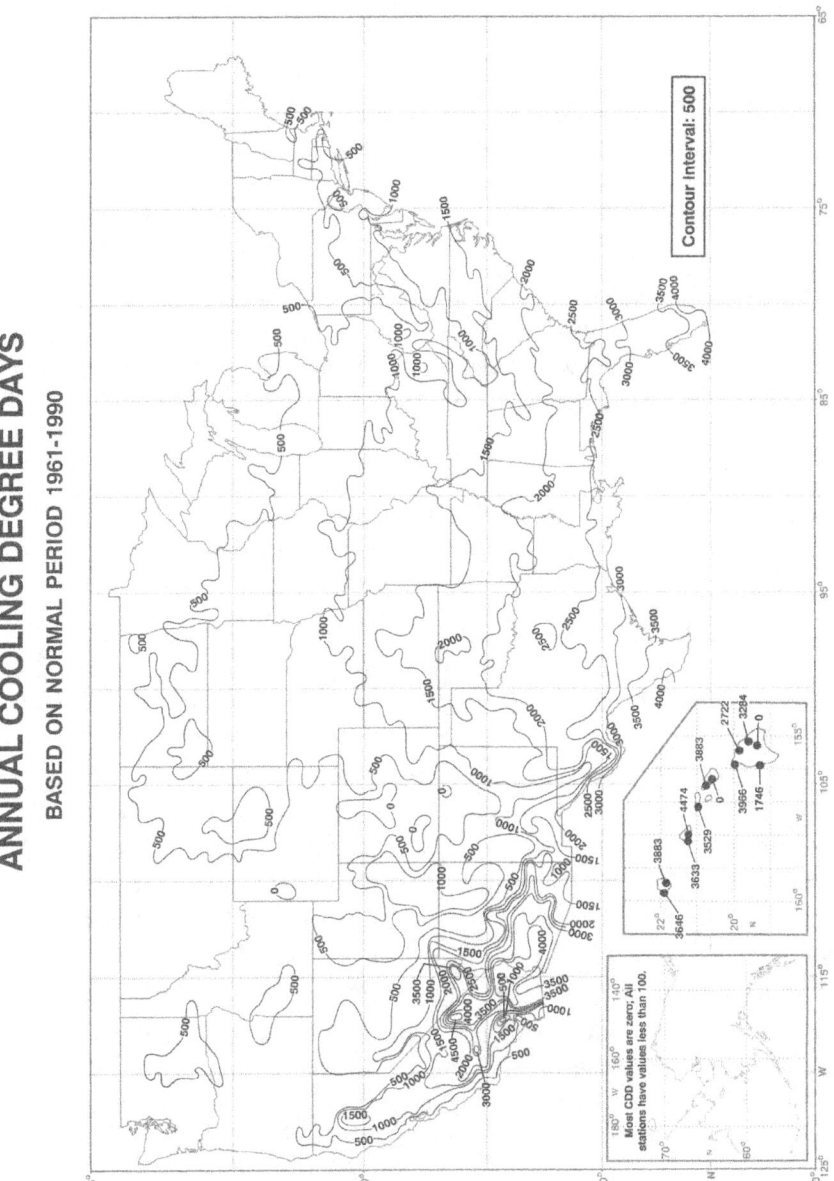

Source: National Climatic Data Center[10]

Average Annual Precipitation and Drought

The amount of rainfall an area receives gives us an idea of whether it will be easy to grow food plants, but there are other reasons to appreciate rainfall. If we are not planning on starting a garden at the potential Bug Out Location, enough rain will allow the growth of wild food and game, and allow us to collect water for drinking.

I have provided a table ranking the states by average annual precipitation. This gives us a general idea of the rainfall of a particular state, but we need more information to find the food-growing potential of the whole state. Precipitation includes snowfall, which doesn't help us grow annual crops and some states are so large that average state precipitation data can be marginalized. Western Montana gets a lot more rainfall than eastern Montana, yet the two regions are lumped together in the state average.

For this reason, I'm including Drought Index Maps, which I find useful because they indicate the degree of dryness of the soil. I think we can get a good idea of the rainfall of an area by looking at those maps.

The maps are updated monthly at the National Climatic Data Center[11] and are based on the Palmer Drought Index. The Palmer Drought Index is a complicated algorithm created to determine whether the soil has enough moisture based on recent precipitation and temperature. The Drought Index uses numbers to indicate the moisture of the soil with a baseline of zero. Negative numbers indicate the soil is in a drought state. Negative one (light red in the maps) indicates mild drought and -4 (dark red in the maps) indicates severe drought.

The best thing about the drought maps is that the data is more finely detailed than the state level, and individual regions of states can be analyzed.

I am providing the maps here for several months throughout the growing season so we can get a 'high level' view of drought potential during the times when we want to grow plants.

The precipitation tables are used as a factor in ranking the states and data was obtained from the National Climatic Data Center[4].

Drought information does not affect the ranking of the states, and the maps supplied here are provided as more information for the reader.

Table: States Ranked by Average Annual Precipitation

Rank	State	Precipitation (inches per year)	Score	Rank	State	Precipitation (inches per year)	Score
1	Louisiana	59.15	100	26	Missouri	42.52	50
2	Mississippi	56.48	98	27	Indiana	41.86	48
3	Alabama	56.00	96	28	Ohio	39.24	46
4	Florida	54.73	94	29	Washington	38.67	44
5	Tennessee	51.85	92	30	Illinois	38.52	42
6	Hawaii	50.33	90	31	Oklahoma	37.62	40
7	Georgia	50.22	88	32	Texas	35.00	38
8	Connecticut	50.07	86	33	Iowa	34.50	36
9	Rhode Island	49.96	84	34	Wisconsin	33.11	34
10	Arkansas	49.72	82	35	Michigan	32.79	32
11	South Carolina	49.24	80	36	Kansas	32.43	30
12	Massachusetts	48.42	78	37	Alaska	29.03	28
13	New Jersey	48.02	76	38	Minnesota	28.61	26
14	North Carolina	46.92	74	39	Nebraska	26.66	24
15	Kentucky	46.27	72	40	California	22.97	22
16	Delaware	45.82	70	41	South Dakota	22.02	20
17	Maine	45.49	68	42	North Dakota	18.59	18
18	New Hampshire	44.84	66	43	Colorado	16.98	16
19	West Virginia	44.36	64	44	Idaho	16.91	14
20	Oregon	43.62	62	45	Utah	15.79	12
21	New York	42.87	60	46	Montana	14.92	10
22	Pennsylvania	42.77	58	47	New Mexico	14.24	8
23	Virginia	42.76	56	48	Wyoming	13.23	6
24	Maryland	42.70	54	49	Arizona	11.80	4
25	Vermont	42.58	52	50	Nevada	9.46	2

Source: National Climatic Data Center[4]

Map: States Ranked by Average Annual Precipitation

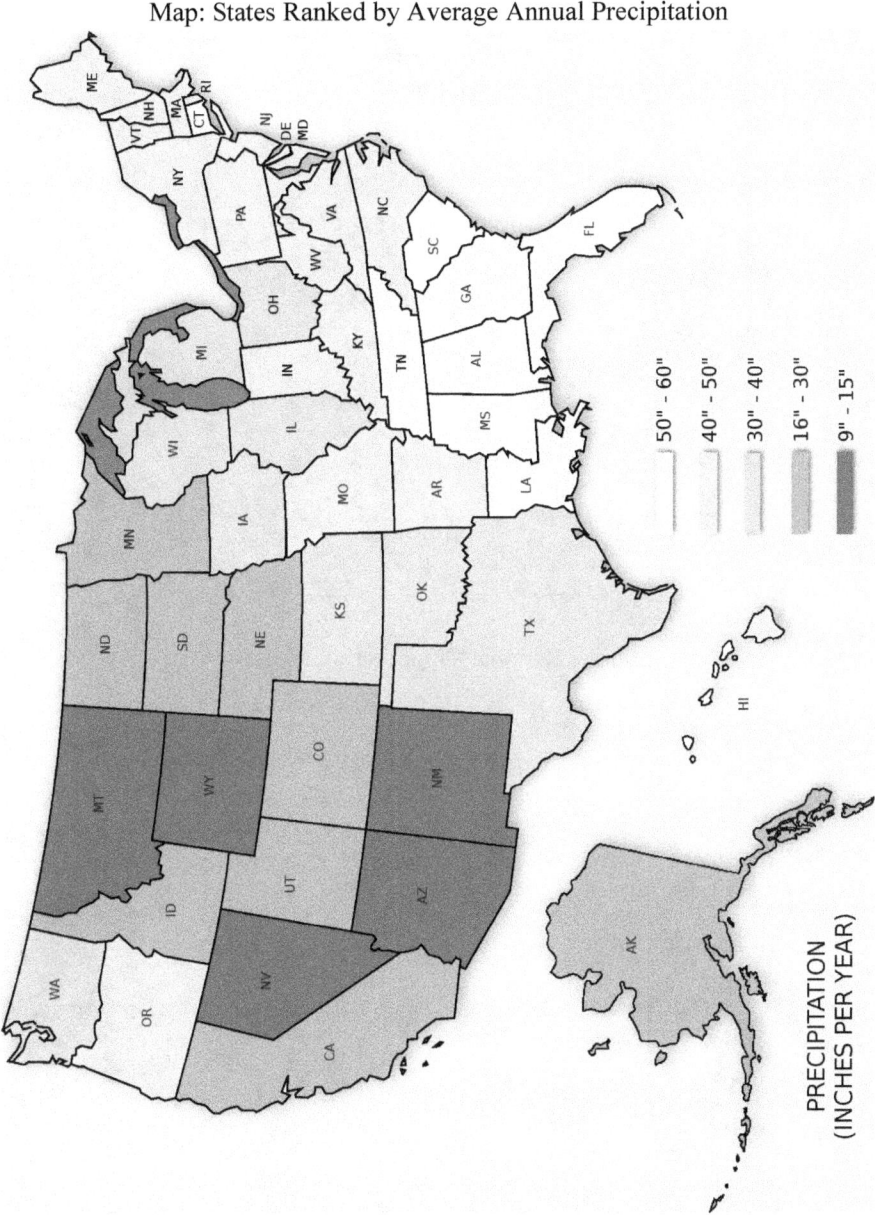

Source: National Climatic Data Center[4]

Map: Drought Index, June

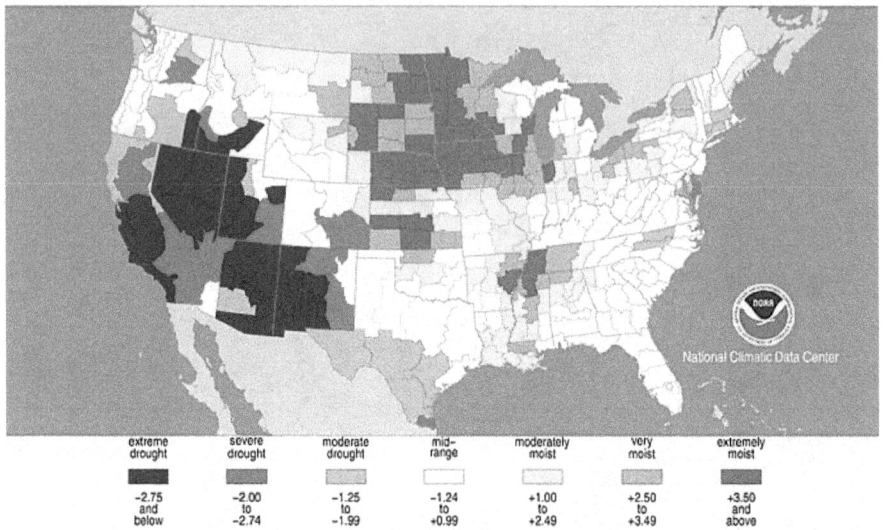

Source: National Climatic Data Center[11]

Map: Drought Index, July

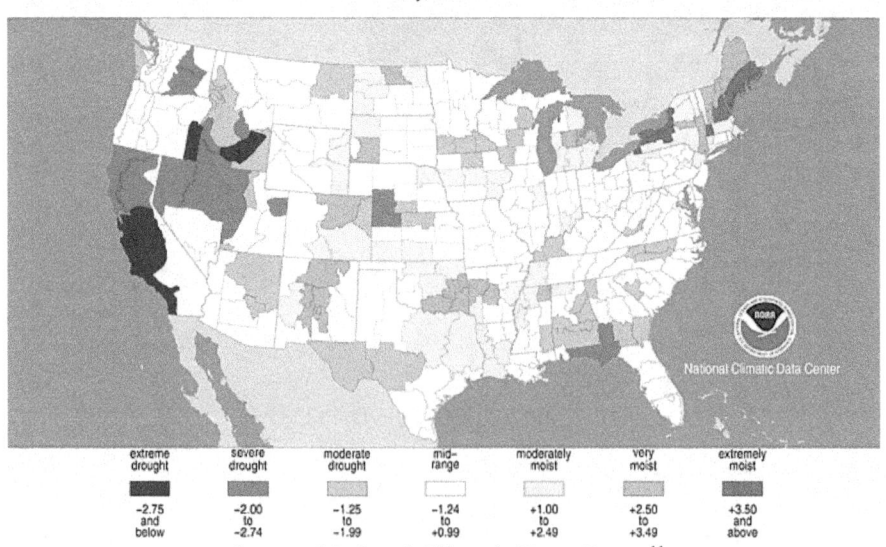

Source: National Climatic Data Center[11]

Map: Drought Index, August

Palmer Z–Index

August, 2014

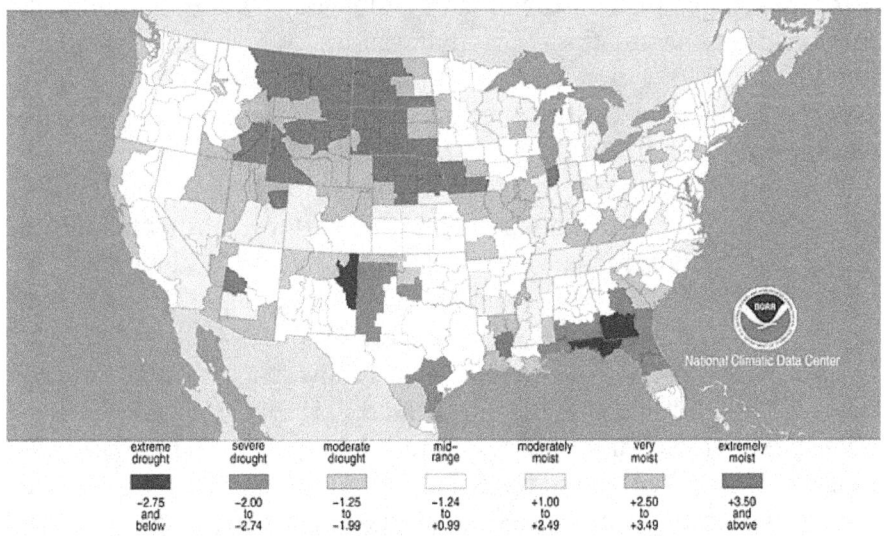

Source: National Climatic Data Center[11]

Map: Drought Index, September

Palmer Z–Index

September, 2014

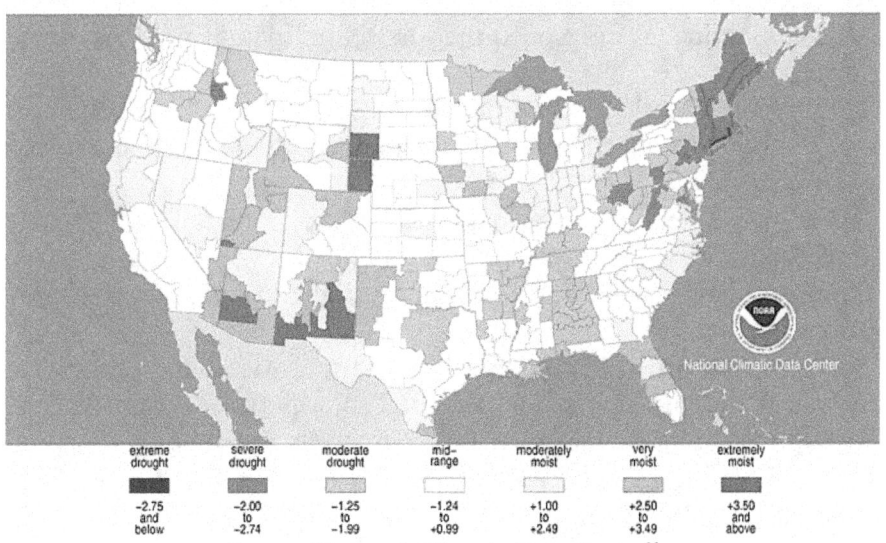

Source: National Climatic Data Center[11]

Renewable Energy

One purpose of the Bug Out Location is to allow us to survive in a grid-down situation. For that reason, we should consider a local renewable energy source. While we don't need electricity to survive, it does make things easier, and in a desperate situation it can improve morale and the *will to live*.

The included maps indicate the solar potential, wind power potential and woody biomass potential of the continental United States and are provided as additional information for the reader.

Solar Power & Wind Power

We don't need to install our renewable energy solution *immediately*, but we should try to find a Bug Out Location with the potential to make improvements at some point. If our Bug Out Location is located on the north side of a mountain, we can assume we are not going to have a good source of solar power, ever. (And it can make it harder to grow food!) But if it has consistent wind, perhaps a wind turbine can be used to generate electricity.

The reader can view the "Average Annual Solar Resource Map" included in this book to get a quick visual indicator of the relative potential solar power in different areas of the country and the Average Annual Wind Speed map to get an idea of potential wind power.

For more detailed maps indicating Solar Power Potential, visit the National Renewable Energy Laboratory's Solar Maps[12] web site.

For more detailed information on wind potential at the state level, visit the U.S. Department of Energy *WIND Exchange*[13] web site or the National Renewable Energy Laboratory's Wind Maps[14] web site.

Renewable Energy Potential information affects the ranking of the states, at least in terms of potential solar power. I quantified the solar power data in the Yearly Average Hours of Solar Potential table. The table lists the annual average daily hours of productive sunlight for solar panels.

Renewable Biomass

The Bug Out Location will need a source of firewood for cooking at the very least, and possibly for heating. Timber can also be used to build structures and fences. I have a sawmill on my own property and it's a good feeling to be able to fell a tree, take it to the sawmill and cut boards for shelves, beams, or even 2x4s. I also have a chain saw mill and it is useful for making long beams. For more information about renewable biomass and more detailed maps, visit ESRI's "Woods Hole US Biomass"[15] web site or the National Renewable Energy Laboratory's Biomass Maps[16] web site.

Map: Average Annual Solar Resource

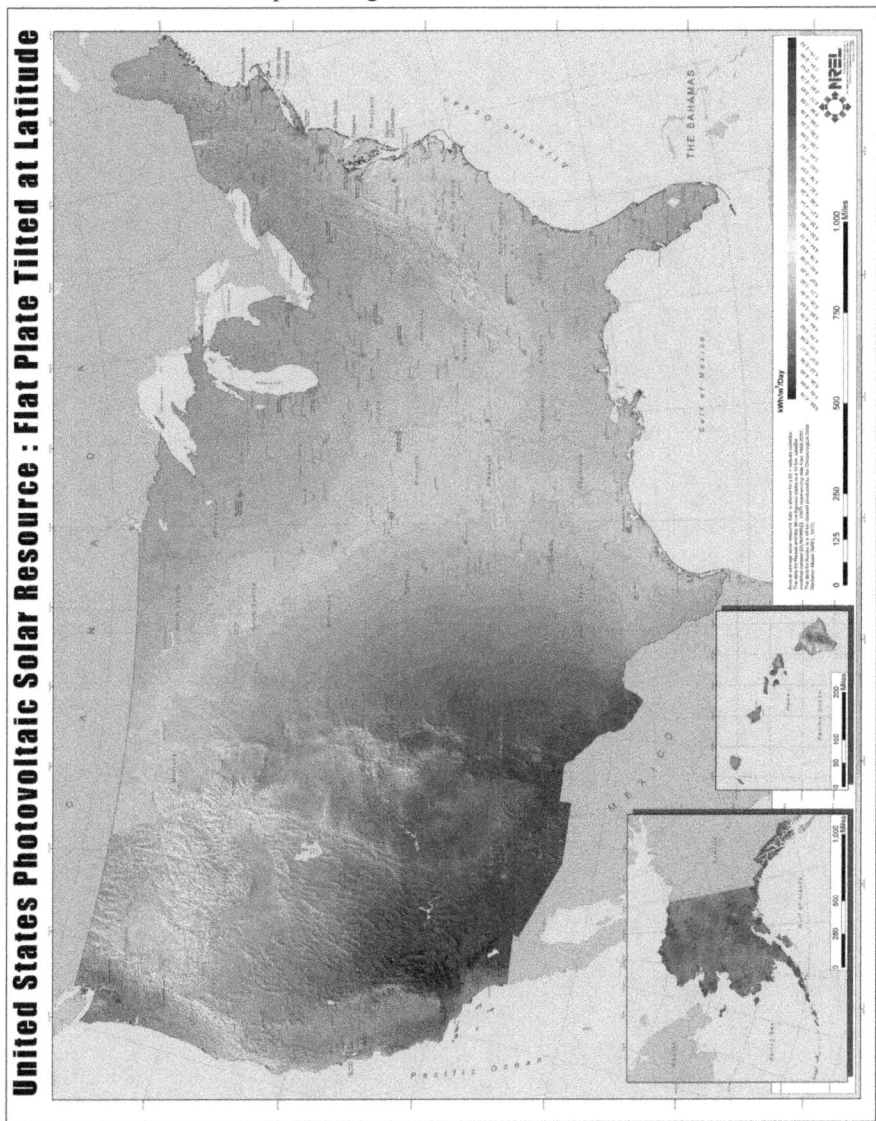

Source: National Renewable Energy Laboratory[12]

Map: Average Annual Wind Speed

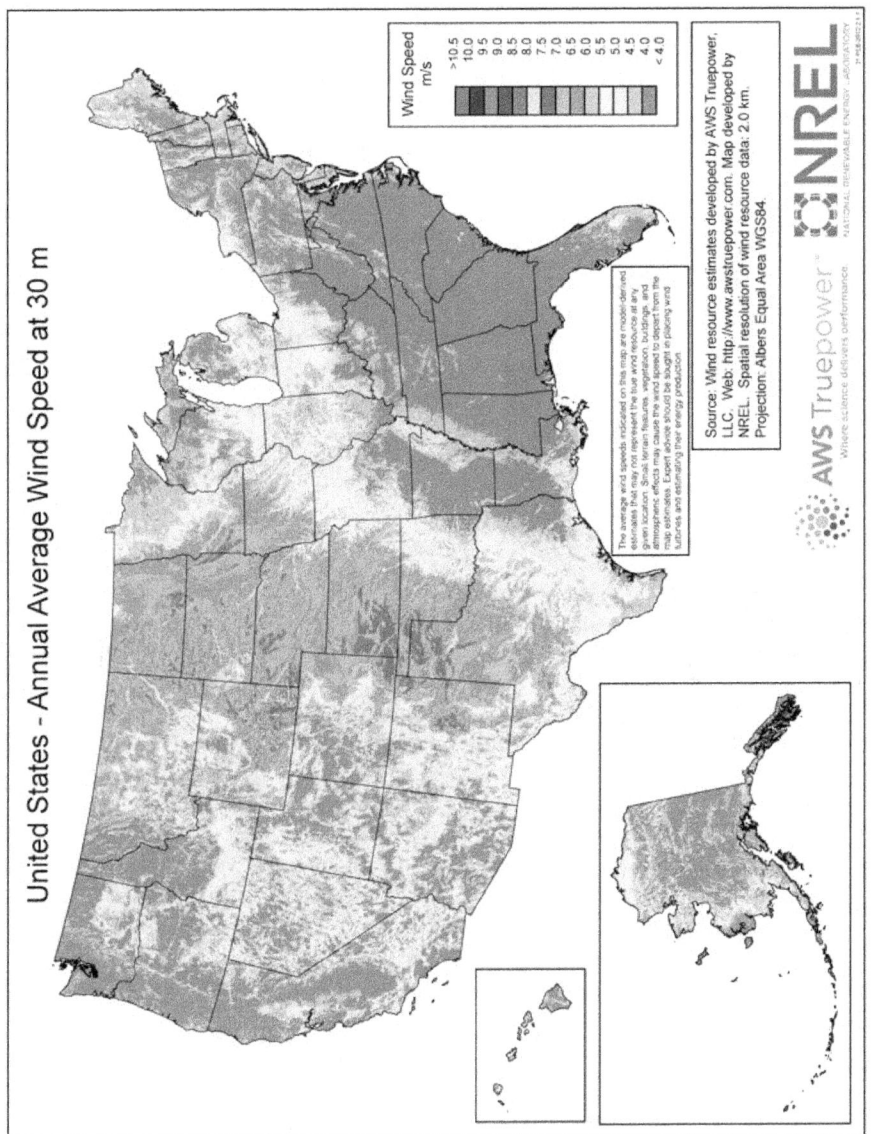

Source: National Renewable Energy Laboratory[14]

Opposite page map credit: NASA Earth Observatory map by Robert Simmon, based on multiple data sets compiled and analyzed by the Woods Hole Research Center. Data inputs include the Shuttle Radar Topography Mission, the National Land Cover Database (based on Landsat) and the Forest Inventory and Analysis of the U.S. Forest Service.

Map: Above Ground Woody Biomass

Source: "NASA Visible Earth: Where the Trees Are."[17]

Table: States Ranked By Solar Power Potential

Rank	State	Year Avg. Hours of Solar Potential	Score	Rank	State	Year Avg. Hours of Solar Potential	Score
1	California	5.22	100	26	Maine	3.23	50
2	Arizona	5.13	98	27	Missouri	3.17	48
3	Texas	4.93	96	28	New York	3.15	46
4	Florida	4.67	94	29	South Dakota	3.12	44
5	New Hampshire	4.61	92	30	Alaska	3.09	42
6	Colorado	4.50	90	31	Michigan	3.07	40
7	Nevada	4.46	88	32	Ohio	3.03	38
8	Utah	4.03	86	32	South Carolina	3.03	38
9	Connecticut	4.00	84	34	North Dakota	3.01	34
10	New Mexico	3.89	82	35	Delaware	3.00	32
11	Washington	3.87	80	36	Kentucky	2.97	30
12	Louisiana	3.87	78	37	Arkansas	2.85	28
13	Oklahoma	3.86	76	38	Minnesota	2.77	26
14	Kansas	3.79	74	39	Maryland	2.74	24
15	Montana	3.77	72	40	Pennsylvania	2.73	22
16	North Carolina	3.67	70	41	Mississippi	2.72	20
17	Georgia	3.58	68	42	Iowa	2.70	18
18	Nebraska	3.56	66	43	Wisconsin	2.65	16
19	Idaho	3.54	64	44	Alabama	2.62	14
20	Wyoming	3.53	62	44	Rhode Island	2.62	14
21	Hawaii	3.51	60	46	Indiana	2.61	10
22	Vermont	3.50	58	46	New Jersey	2.61	10
23	Massachusetts	3.46	56	48	Virginia	2.57	6
24	Oregon	3.32	54	49	West Virginia	2.33	4
25	Tennessee	3.27	52	50	Illinois	2.07	2

Source: National Renewable Energy Laboratory[12]

Map: States Ranked By Solar Power Potential

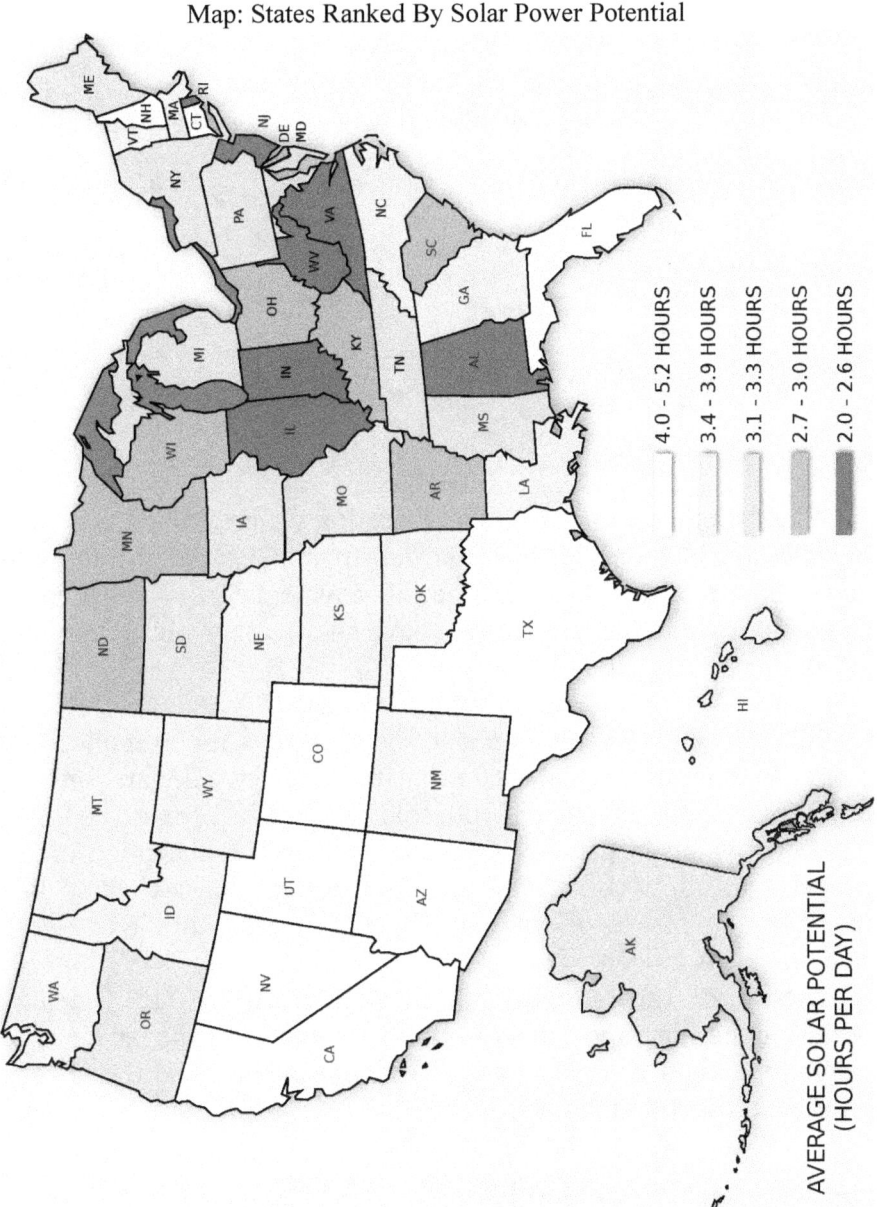

Source: Source: National Renewable Energy Laboratory[12]

Economy

To rank the states I am including economic data from eight different categories:

1. Taxes
2. Cost of Living
3. Income
4. Government Assistance
5. Unemployment Rate
6. Cost of Buying a Home

Taxes

When shopping for a Bug Out Location we need to consider the big picture. Not only population density but Cost of Living and taxes. The impact of taxes can be felt now or later (or both) but at some point your state's taxes will have an effect on your life.

Property Sales Tax

Taxes may also affect the sale of property - for example New York State imposes a real estate transfer tax of two dollars for each $500. This amounts to a $100 sales tax on a property sold at $50,000, which is paid by the seller who raises the price of his property to allow for it. One hundred dollars doesn't sound like much, but it makes one wonder in what other ways New York State taxes its citizens.

There are other types of taxes to consider. If you buy undeveloped land and intend to build a cabin on it the presence of sales taxes (and a higher cost of living) can increase the cost of your construction materials.

Retirement Income Taxes

Other taxes depend on specific situations. Normally you won't pay income taxes in a state in which you don't reside, and many states allow property tax exemptions for retired folks. At the time of this writing there are only three states; Delaware, Missouri, and Rhode Island, that *don't have* some type of property tax exemption for disabled veterans. Some states sound like they would be perfect for a Bug Out Location but aren't tax-friendly to retirees - for example Montana, Oregon, Nebraska and Minnesota. On the other hand, South Dakota and Wyoming are very tax-friendly to retirees. Even if you're not retired at this time its better to think ahead - someday you will be (hopefully!)

But retiree taxes should not be the only taxes to consider. Each state may be advantageous in other tax areas. For example, while Montana taxes most forms of retirement income, there is no state sales tax and their combined average annual state and local taxes are 5% less than the national average. (To put it into perspective, New York state is 39% above the national average and Wyoming is 66% below the national average.)

There is another way to view retiree taxes vs sales tax. If your only income source is retirement income and you plan to buy your Bug Out Location outright, retire to immediately it and not spend much money for the rest of your days, you might be better off finding a Bug Out Location in Wyoming which has no income tax (on regular income, Social Security income or retirement income) and a 4% sales tax (food and prescription drugs are exempt). On the other hand, if you are young and plan on buying a piece of bare land and building a homestead on it, you may be better off in a state like Montana which has no sales tax and an income tax rate of 6.9% on income above $16,700.

Income Taxes

There are seven states without state income taxes and some of these should be strongly considered. They are Alaska, Florida, Nevada, South Dakota, Texas, Washington and Wyoming. Incidentally, these states have other features which rank them high on the list of states to consider. (Tennessee and New Hampshire have an income tax low enough that they may be considered nil, but they do tax interest and dividends which can affect retirees.)

How do theses states manage to avoid an income tax? Usually by increasing other taxes:

- Alaska also has no state sales tax and a relatively low property tax rate! The state is funded mostly through its booming oil and gas production, which benefits residents directly in the form of an average $1,100 payout to every resident each year.

• Florida funds itself with a high sales tax (6%) and high property taxes. In terms of overall taxes Florida ranks about middle of the road compared to other states.

• Nevada has a high sales tax rate which starts at 6.85% but overall is tax friendly to its citizens.

• South Dakota has a 4% sales tax and various use taxes, but like Nevada has a relatively low overall tax rate.

• Texas has a 6.25% sales tax rate and like Alaska is helped by the oil and gas industry. Overall Texas has a relatively low tax rate.

• Washington state has a 6.5% sales tax and localities can add to that so in some areas the sales tax is as high as 9.5%. It charges businesses at a rate of 1% of their revenue, so even businesses losing money are taxed. In addition, property taxes are very high. All of which makes Washington one of the least tax-friendly states in the union.

• Wyoming has a 4% sales tax and a property tax rate which varies depending on the locality.

• Tennessee has no income tax but has a 7% sales tax and a 6% tax on interest and dividends making it undesirable for retirees.

• New Hampshire taxes interest and dividends at 5% and has high property taxes, also making it undesirable for retirees.

For purposes of ranking the states, they are ranked in order of Per Capita State & Local Tax Burden. Data was obtained from the U.S. Bureau of Economic Analysis[18].

Map: States Ranked by State & Local Taxes

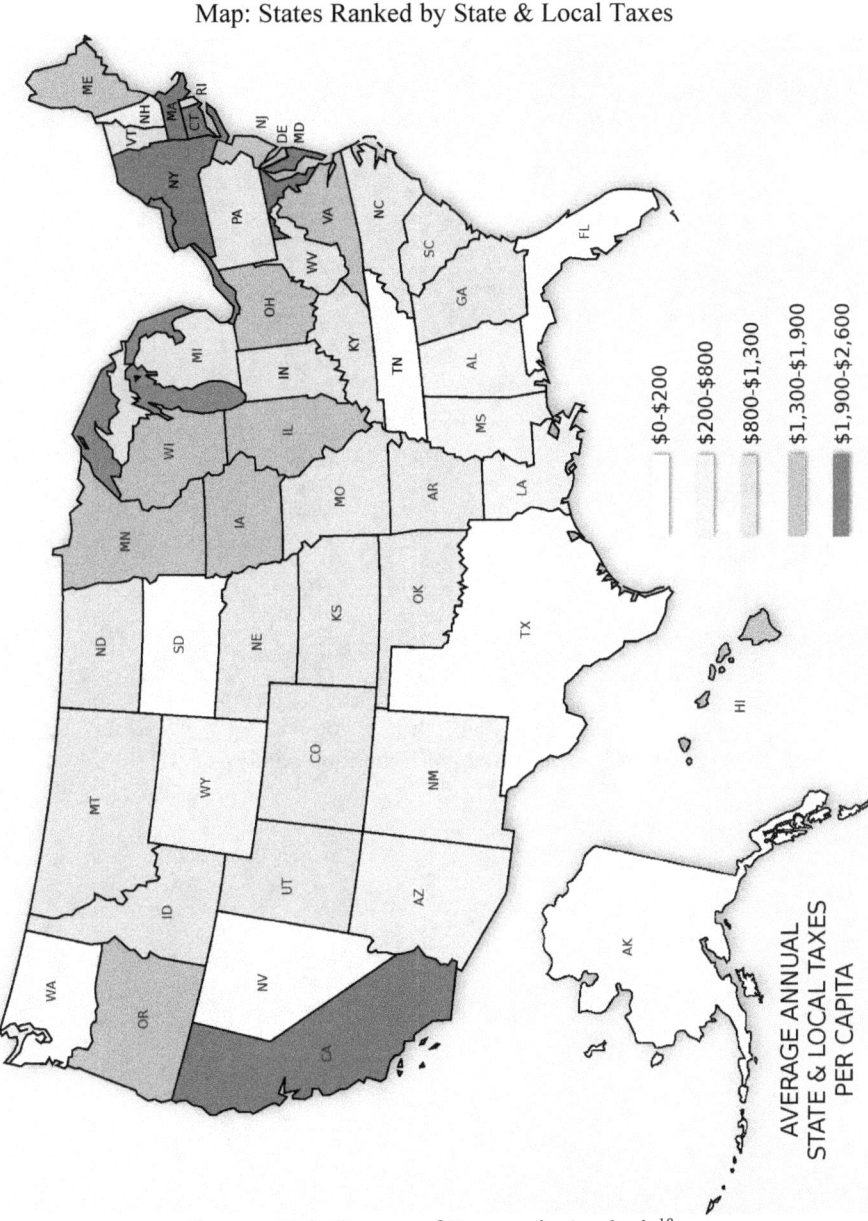

Source: U.S. Bureau of Economic Analysis[18]

Table: States Ranked by State & Local Taxes

Rank	State	Per Capita State & Local Tax Burden	Score	Rank	State	Per Capita State & Local Tax Burden	Score
1	Florida	$68	100	26	Kansas	$1,162	50
2	Texas	$89	98	27	Vermont	$1,189	48
3	Tennessee	$100	96	28	Montana	$1,199	46
4	Nevada	$114	94	29	Kentucky	$1,205	44
5	Washington	$122	92	30	Colorado	$1,210	42
6	Alaska	$125	90	31	Rhode Island	$1,216	40
7	South Dakota	$125	88	32	North Carolina	$1,230	38
8	New Hampshire	$205	86	33	Pennsylvania	$1,285	36
9	Wyoming	$239	84	34	Nebraska	$1,298	34
10	Arizona	$597	82	35	Maine	$1,302	32
11	Louisiana	$627	80	36	Iowa	$1,310	30
12	New Mexico	$654	78	37	Ohio	$1,340	28
13	Mississippi	$704	76	38	Wisconsin	$1,359	26
14	Alabama	$788	74	39	Delaware	$1,362	24
15	South Carolina	$829	72	40	Hawaii	$1,383	22
16	Idaho	$905	70	41	Illinois	$1,413	20
17	Oklahoma	$906	68	42	New Jersey	$1,444	18
18	Georgia	$979	66	43	Virginia	$1,487	16
19	Arkansas	$992	64	44	Oregon	$1,699	14
20	Michigan	$1,027	62	45	Minnesota	$1,850	12
21	North Dakota	$1,031	60	46	California	$1,911	10
22	West Virginia	$1,056	58	47	Massachusetts	$2,127	8
23	Utah	$1,075	56	48	Maryland	$2,167	6
24	Missouri	$1,078	54	49	Connecticut	$2,361	4
25	Indiana	$1,129	52	50	New York	$2,610	2

Source: U.S. Bureau of Economic Analysis[18]

Cost of Living

Another thing to consider, especially if you will be living at your Survival Homestead, is that the local cost of living has a direct relationship to your income. If your Survival Homestead is in a high cost of living state such as Virginia but you reside and work in a lower cost of living state such as Tennessee you will find that your paycheck won't go as far when buying materials or food in Virginia to establish your homestead.

"Cost of living" can be defined as the real cost of working and residing in an area. Categories that make up the cost of living in this book include rent, food, child care, transportation, health care, taxes and "other necessities". "Other necessities" includes apparel, entertainment, personal care products and services, reading, education, and miscellaneous items.

To find a detailed cost of living report for a state's different cities or rural areas, visit the "Economic Policy Institute 2013 Family Budget Calculator"[19] at their web site: http://www.epi.org/resources/budget.

Cost of living data was used to rank the states and the data was obtained from the U.S. Bureau of Economic Analysis[18].

Table: States Ranked By Cost Of Living

Rank	State	Cost of Living	Score	Rank	State	Cost of Living	Score
1	Arkansas	$37,502	100	26	New Mexico	$44,288	50
2	Tennessee	$37,518	98	27	Michigan	$44,790	48
3	Mississippi	$37,912	96	28	Nevada	$44,803	46
4	Missouri	$39,330	94	29	Wisconsin	$44,935	44
5	Georgia	$39,346	92	30	Pennsylvania	$45,152	42
6	Kentucky	$39,607	90	31	North Carolina	$45,239	40
7	Idaho	$39,848	88	32	Washington	$45,403	38
8	Oklahoma	$39,896	86	33	Montana	$45,671	36
9	Louisiana	$40,098	84	34	Minnesota	$45,854	34
10	Kansas	$40,420	82	35	New York	$46,871	32
11	North Dakota	$40,425	80	36	Wyoming	$47,142	30
12	Ohio	$40,799	78	37	Illinois	$47,701	28
13	Texas	$40,991	76	38	Maine	$48,102	26
14	South Dakota	$41,031	74	39	Colorado	$49,581	24
15	South Carolina	$41,205	72	40	Maryland	$49,583	22
16	Alabama	$41,376	70	41	California	$50,900	20
17	West Virginia	$41,842	68	42	Delaware	$51,820	18
18	Iowa	$41,865	66	43	Vermont	$52,976	16
19	Oregon	$43,420	64	44	Alaska	$54,583	14
20	Florida	$43,473	62	45	Rhode Island	$54,881	12
21	Utah	$43,617	60	46	New Hampshire	$55,059	10
22	Arizona	$43,710	58	47	Hawaii	$56,111	8
23	Indiana	$43,797	56	48	New Jersey	$57,478	6
24	Virginia	$43,860	54	49	Massachusetts	$57,953	4
25	Nebraska	$43,933	52	50	Connecticut	$59,668	2

Source: U.S. Bureau of Economic Analysis[18]

Map: States Ranked By Cost Of Living

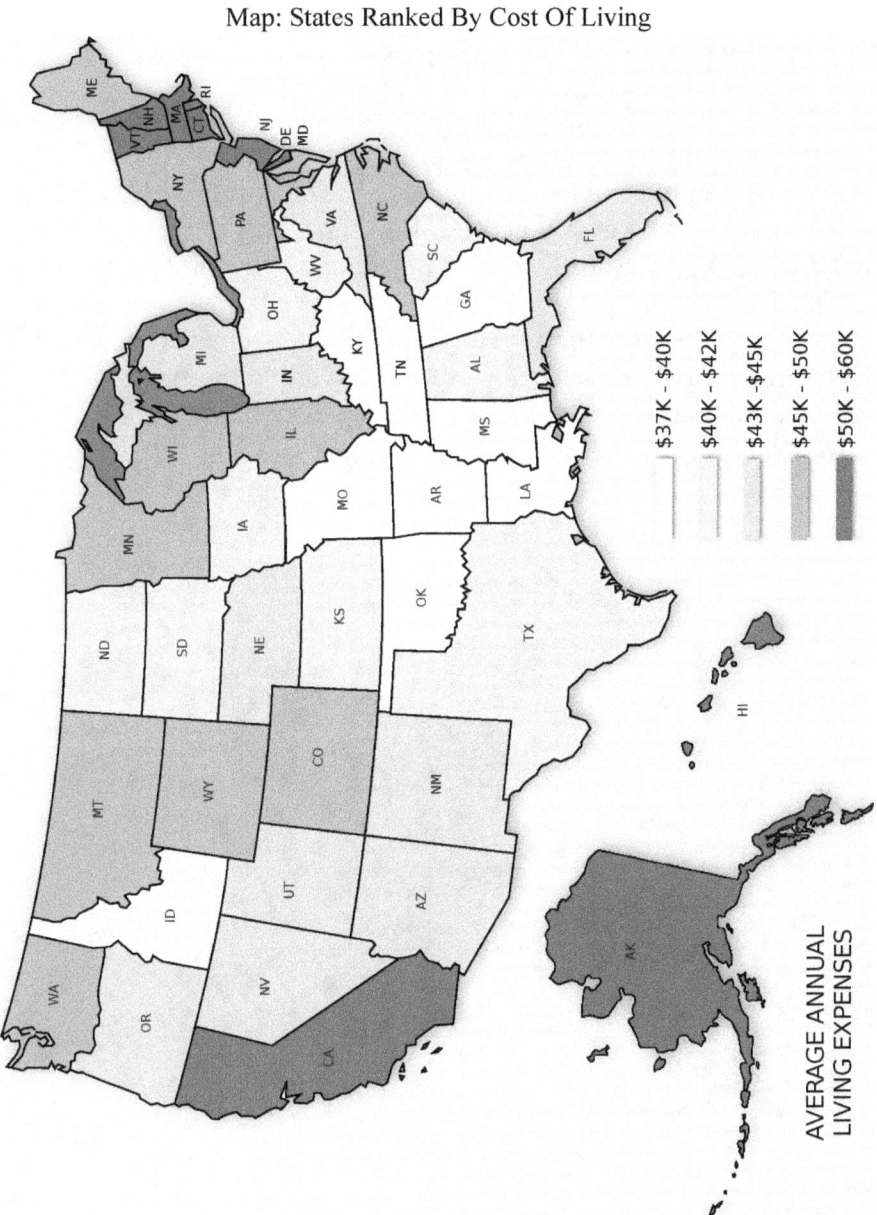

Source: U.S. Bureau of Economic Analysis[18]

Income

The income level of a state can reflect the ability to make a living wage, but it should be compared to the cost of living of the state. You can make a lot more money in California, but real estate prices and the cost of living are a lot higher in California, so your income might go no further than if you chose a Bug Out Location in Oklahoma.

Income levels for the ranking table was obtained from the U.S. Department of Commerce and Bureau of Economic Analysis[18] and the income numbers used are per capita.

Map: States Ranked By Income

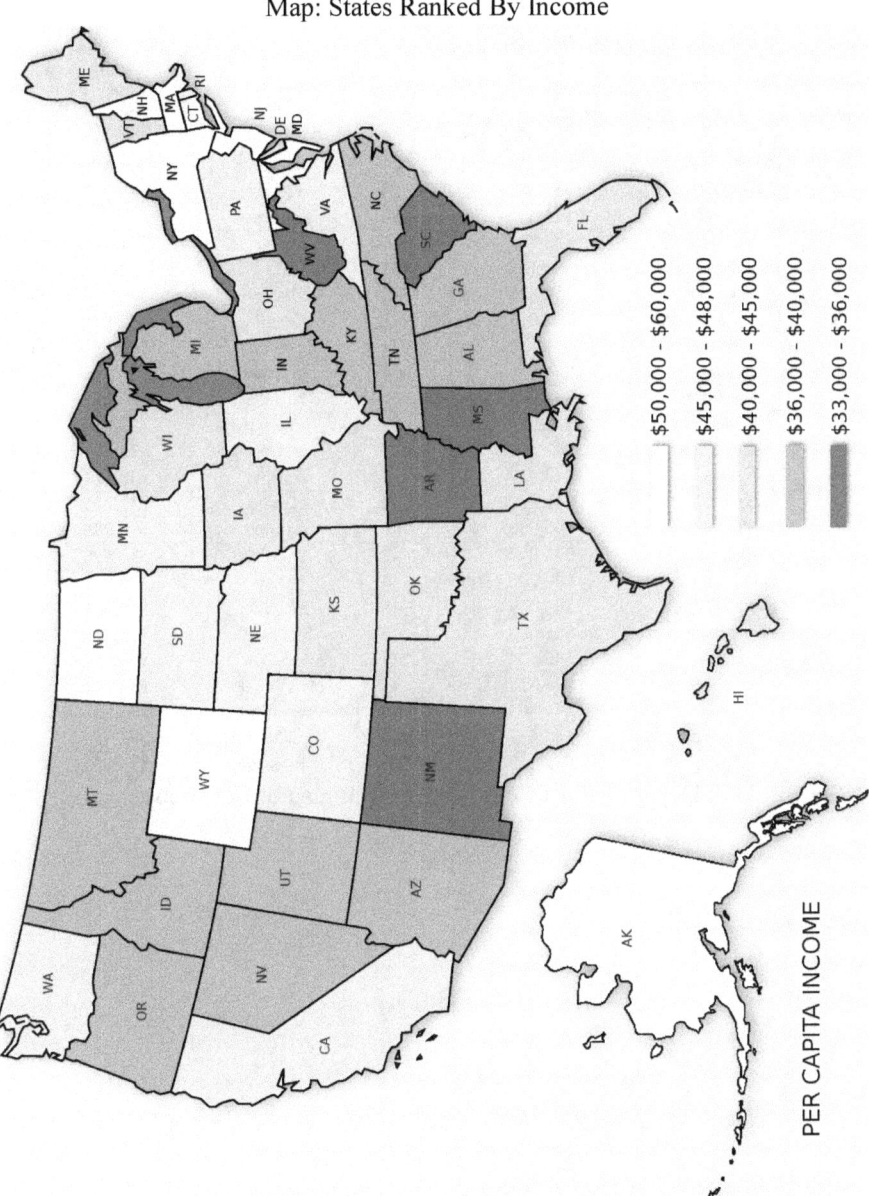

Source: U.S. Department of Commerce and Bureau of Economic Analysis[18]

Table: States Ranked By Income

Rank	State	Per capita personal income (dollars)	Score	Rank	State	Per capita personal income (dollars)	Score
1	Connecticut	$60,658	100	26	Wisconsin	$43,244	50
2	Massachusetts	$57,248	98	27	Oklahoma	$41,861	48
3	New Jersey	$55,386	96	28	Florida	$41,497	46
4	New York	$54,462	94	29	Louisiana	$41,204	44
5	Maryland	$53,826	92	30	Ohio	$41,049	42
6	North Dakota	$53,182	90	31	Maine	$40,924	40
7	Wyoming	$52,826	88	32	Missouri	$40,663	38
8	New Hampshire	$51,013	86	33	Oregon	$39,848	36
9	Alaska	$50,150	84	34	Tennessee	$39,558	34
10	Virginia	$48,838	82	35	Montana	$39,366	32
11	California	$48,434	80	36	Nevada	$39,235	30
12	Washington	$47,717	78	37	Michigan	$39,055	28
13	Minnesota	$47,500	76	38	North Carolina	$38,683	26
14	Nebraska	$47,157	74	39	Indiana	$38,622	24
15	Rhode Island	$46,989	72	40	Georgia	$37,845	22
16	Illinois	$46,980	70	41	Arizona	$36,983	20
17	Colorado	$46,897	68	42	Arkansas	$36,698	18
18	Pennsylvania	$46,202	66	43	Utah	$36,640	16
19	South Dakota	$46,039	64	44	Alabama	$36,481	14
20	Vermont	$45,483	62	45	Kentucky	$36,214	12
21	Hawaii	$45,204	60	46	Idaho	$36,146	10
22	Delaware	$44,815	58	47	New Mexico	$35,965	8
23	Iowa	$44,763	56	48	South Carolina	$35,831	6
24	Kansas	$44,417	54	49	West Virginia	$35,533	4
25	Texas	$43,862	52	50	Mississippi	$33,913	2

Source: U.S. Department of Commerce and Bureau of Economic Analysis[18]

Government Assistance

I included government assistance in the ranking of the states because in addition to being an economic indicator, it may indicate the attitude of a state's citizens. It makes sense that we would want to locate our Bug Out Location or Survival Homestead in an area where the people are self-reliant and independent.

West Virginia is a good example of this attitude. Although the state ranks 49th in income, it ranks only 13th in percentage of residents receiving welfare. This indicates that although the people in that state are poorer than most of the rest of the country, they are proud and determined to get by without help from the government. Those are the kind of people we should want around us when times get bad.

While both "% on Welfare" and "Medicaid Spending" are listed in the tables, only welfare is used to rank the states.

The data was obtained from the U.S. Bureau of Economic Analysis[18].

Table: States Ranked by Government Assistance

Rank	State	% on Welfare	Medicaid Spending	Score	Rank	State	% on Welfare	Medicaid Spending	Score
1	Louisiana	1.5%	$8,616	50	26	Kentucky	2.8%	$9,607	25
1	North Dakota	1.5%	$23,810	50	26	New Mexico	2.8%	N/A	25
3	South Carolina	1.6%	$10,346	48	28	South Dakota	2.9%	$10,916	23
4	Wyoming	1.7%	$20,726	47	29	Idaho	3.0%	$10,324	22
5	Georgia	1.8%	$7,604	46	29	New Hampshire	3.0%	$18,341	22
5	Texas	1.8%	$9,751	46	29	New Jersey	3.0%	$17,646	22
7	Alabama	1.9%	$8,358	44	32	Connecticut	3.1%	$14,652	19
8	North Carolina	2.0%	$9,157	43	32	Rhode Island	3.1%	$13,820	19
8	Virginia	2.0%	$11,447	43	34	Massachusetts	3.2%	$21,129	17
10	Indiana	2.1%	$14,991	41	34	Nevada	3.2%	$7,169	17
10	Kansas	2.1%	$13,643	41	36	Ohio	3.3%	$19,858	15
10	Nebraska	2.1%	$14,794	41	37	Hawaii	3.4%	$16,432	14
13	Colorado	2.2%	$16,943	38	37	Mississippi	3.4%	$10,347	14
13	West Virginia	2.2%	$14,155	38	37	New York	3.4%	$21,620	14
13	Wisconsin	2.2%	$14,866	38	37	Oklahoma	3.4%	$10,085	14
16	Arizona	2.3%	$12,628	35	37	Tennessee	3.4%	$8,595	14
16	Florida	2.3%	$8,532	35	42	Minnesota	3.7%	$17,053	9
18	Utah	2.4%	$11,624	33	42	Pennsylvania	3.7%	$17,462	9
19	Illinois	2.5%	$9,926	32	44	Michigan	3.9%	$15,403	7
19	Montana	2.5%	$22,543	32	45	Washington	4.0%	$12,140	6
21	Delaware	2.6%	$13,439	30	46	California	4.1%	$11,749	5
21	Iowa	2.6%	$15,865	30	47	Oregon	4.2%	$15,626	4
21	Maryland	2.6%	$16,591	30	48	Vermont	4.6%	$6,405	3
21	Missouri	2.6%	$14,706	30	49	Maine	5.2%	$8,932	2
25	Arkansas	2.7%	$12,994	26	50	Alaska	6.6%	$23,321	1

Source: U.S. Bureau of Economic Analysis[18]

Map: States Ranked by Government Assistance

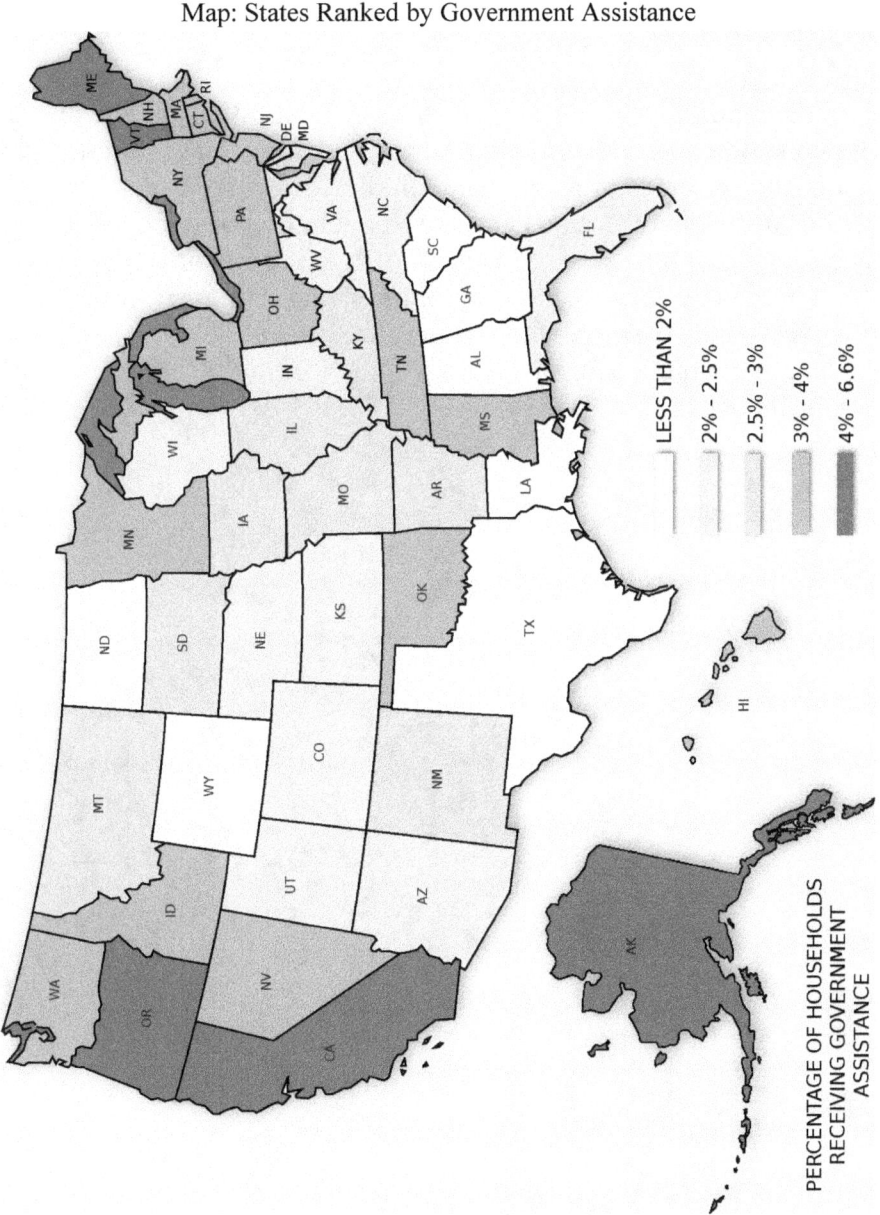

Source: U.S. Bureau of Economic Analysis[18]

Unemployment Rate

The importance of a state's unemployment rate is obvious if we are considering a Survival Homestead, where we may want to find a job. It also serves as an economic indicator.

For more detailed maps and to see unemployment figures at the county level, go to the U.S. Bureau of Labor Statistics *Local Area Unemployment Statistics Information and Analysis* web site: http://data.bls.gov/map/MapToolServlet?survey=la.

Unemployment statistics were obtained from the U.S. Bureau of Labor Statistics[20].

Map: States Ranked by Unemployment

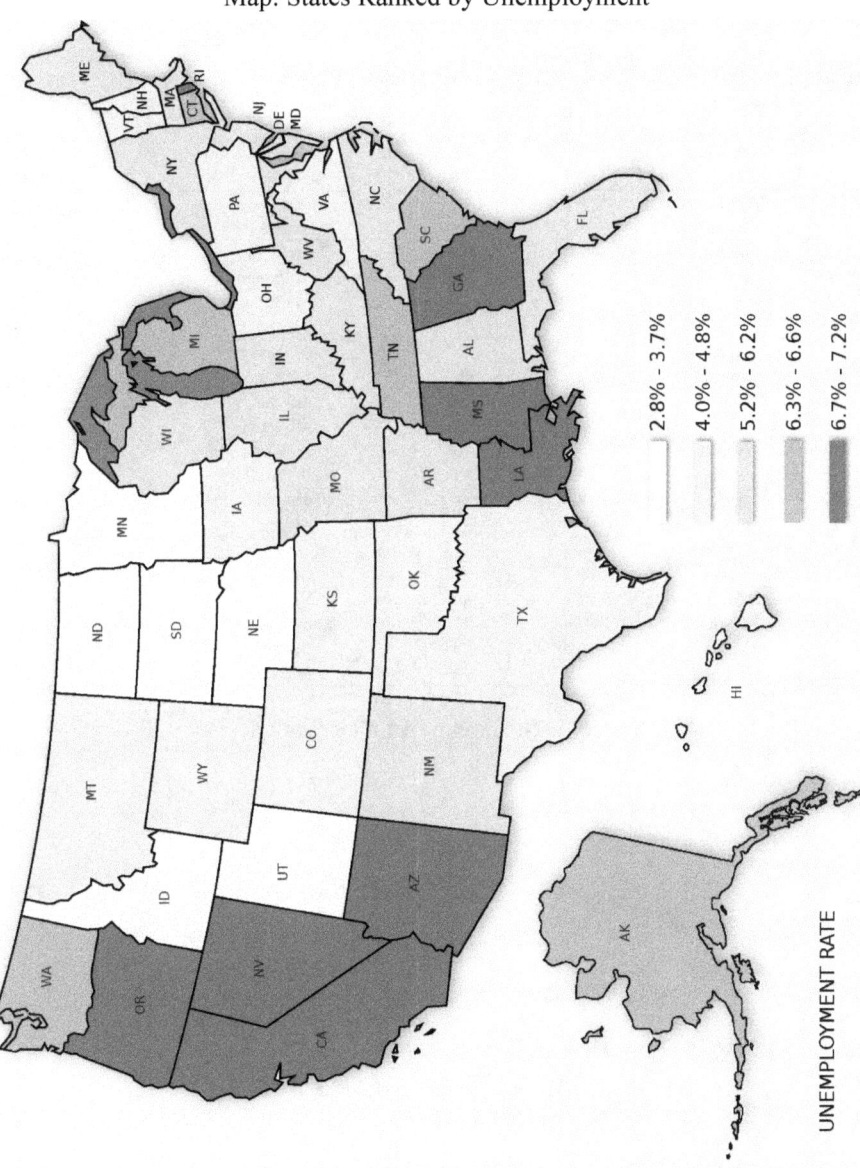

Source: U.S. Bureau of Labor Statistics[20]

Table: States Ranked by Unemployment

Rank	State	Unemployment Rate (%)	Score	Rank	State	Unemployment Rate (%)	Score
1	North Dakota	2.8	50	23	North Carolina	5.5	28
2	Nebraska	2.9	49	27	Florida	5.6	24
3	South Dakota	3.3	48	28	Alabama	5.7	23
4	Utah	3.5	47	28	Arkansas	5.7	23
5	Minnesota	3.6	46	28	Kentucky	5.7	23
6	Idaho	3.7	45	31	Indiana	5.8	20
7	Colorado	4	44	31	New York	5.8	20
7	Hawaii	4	44	33	West Virginia	6	18
7	New Hampshire	4	44	34	New Mexico	6.1	17
10	Iowa	4.1	41	35	Illinois	6.2	16
11	Kansas	4.2	40	35	New Jersey	6.2	16
11	Montana	4.2	40	37	Alaska	6.3	14
11	Oklahoma	4.2	40	37	Michigan	6.3	14
11	Vermont	4.2	40	37	Washington	6.3	14
11	Wyoming	4.2	40	40	Connecticut	6.4	11
16	Texas	4.6	35	41	South Carolina	6.5	10
17	Ohio	4.8	34	42	Tennessee	6.6	9
17	Pennsylvania	4.8	34	43	Arizona	6.7	8
17	Virginia	4.8	34	43	Louisiana	6.7	8
20	Wisconsin	5.2	31	43	Oregon	6.7	8
21	Delaware	5.4	30	46	Nevada	6.8	5
21	Missouri	5.4	30	46	Rhode Island	6.8	5
23	Maine	5.5	28	48	Georgia	6.9	3
23	Maryland	5.5	28	49	California	7	2
23	Massachusetts	5.5	28	50	Mississippi	7.2	1

Source: U.S. Bureau of Labor Statistics[20]

Cost of Buying a Home

Why should we be concerned about the cost of buying a home in our Bug Out state? We may be buying bare land on which to build our Bug Out Location.

But home prices serve as an indicator of real estate prices. Typically if a state has higher home prices, other real estate will also be higher priced. There are exceptions, but generally speaking, Bug Out land in California will be four times more expensive than similar land in West Virginia, as can be seen on the Cost of Buying a Home table.

Cost of buying a home is used to rank the states. Data was obtained from the U.S. Census Bureau[21].

Table: States Ranked By Cost of Buying a Home

Rank	State	Value of Housing Units (rounded)	Score	Rank	State	Value of Housing Units (rounded)	Score
1	Mississippi	$91,000	100	26	Wisconsin	$166,000	50
1	West Virginia	$91,000	100	27	Idaho	$167,000	48
3	Arkansas	$97,000	96	28	Maine	$172,000	46
4	Oklahoma	$99,000	94	29	Illinois	$200,000	44
5	North Dakota	$104,000	92	30	Vermont	$201,000	42
6	Alabama	$112,000	90	31	Minnesota	$207,000	40
7	Kentucky	$113,000	88	32	Utah	$208,000	38
8	South Dakota	$115,000	86	33	Florida	$211,000	36
9	Iowa	$116,000	84	34	Arizona	$218,000	34
10	Kansas	$119,000	82	35	Alaska	$221,000	32
10	Texas	$119,000	82	36	Colorado	$234,000	30
12	Indiana	$120,000	78	37	Delaware	$235,000	28
12	Nebraska	$120,000	78	38	Oregon	$244,000	26
14	Louisiana	$121,000	74	39	Virginia	$247,000	24
15	South Carolina	$128,000	72	40	New Hampshire	$253,000	22
16	Tennessee	$129,000	70	41	Nevada	$275,000	20
17	Missouri	$135,000	68	42	Washington	$278,000	18
17	Ohio	$135,000	68	43	Rhode Island	$284,000	16
19	North Carolina	$144,000	64	44	Connecticut	$296,000	14
20	Michigan	$148,000	62	45	New York	$301,000	12
21	New Mexico	$151,000	60	46	Maryland	$326,000	10
22	Pennsylvania	$152,000	58	47	New Jersey	$357,000	8
23	Georgia	$160,000	56	48	Massachusetts	$358,000	6
24	Montana	$162,000	54	49	California	$479,000	4
25	Wyoming	$163,000	52	50	Hawaii	$522,000	2

Source: U.S. Census Bureau[21]

Map: States Ranked By Cost of Buying a Home

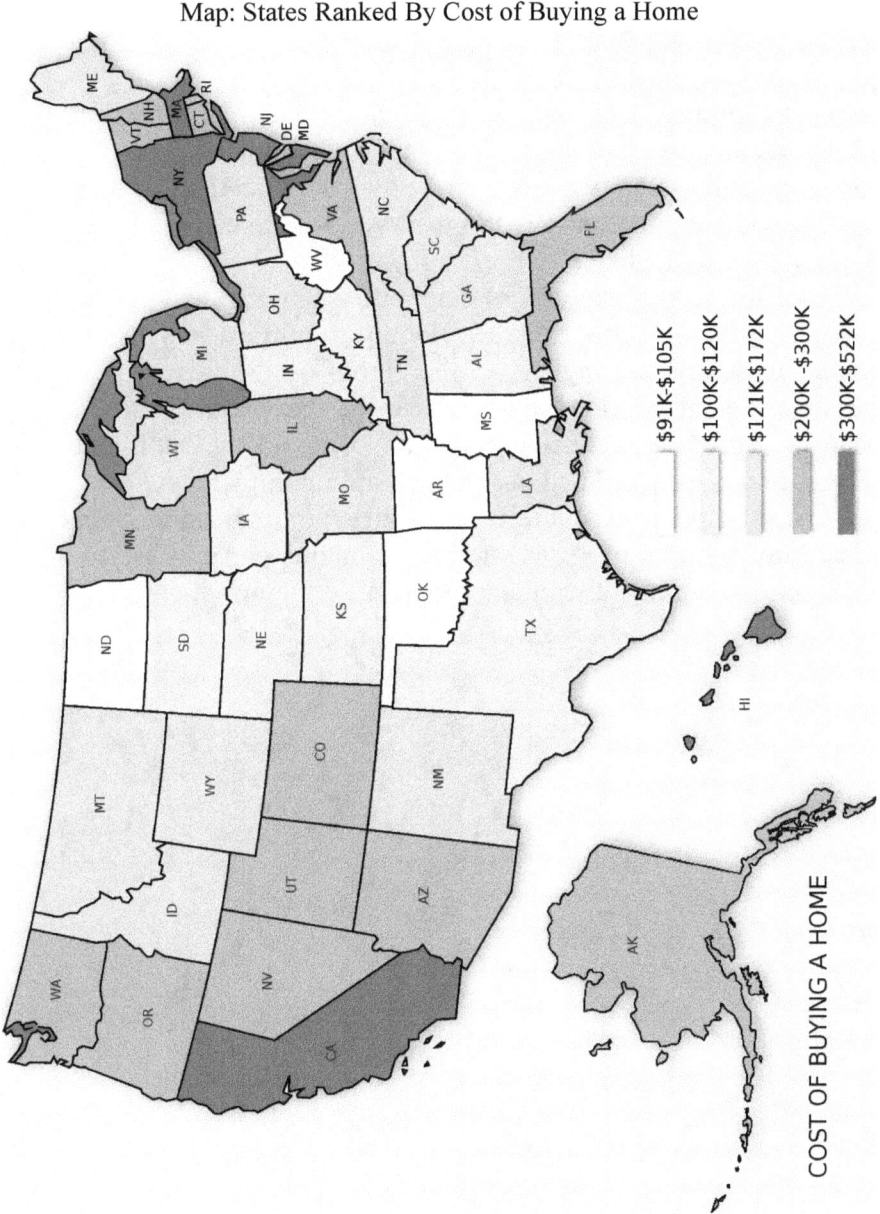

Source: U.S. Census Bureau[21]

Gun Laws

Guns and Bug Out Locations go hand in hand. If we want a Bug Out Location, we probably also want to be able to protect it. We are survivalists, so we probably have a collection of firearms. Maybe we are concerned with preserving the Second Amendment. Or maybe we just like to target shoot!

The gun-friendliness of a state reflects more than simply gun laws. In general, states that are friendly to gun owners also tend to spend less time infringing on the rights of its citizens. For this reason, even if we don't enjoy firearms, the gun-friendliness of a state is important to consider when choosing a Bug Out Location.

Gun laws weighed heavily in the state rankings.

The data presented here is from 2014 and considers Right-To-Carry laws, limits on rifles such as magazine capacity, restrictions of suppressors and adherence of the Castle Doctrine.

Map: States Ranked by Gun Friendliness

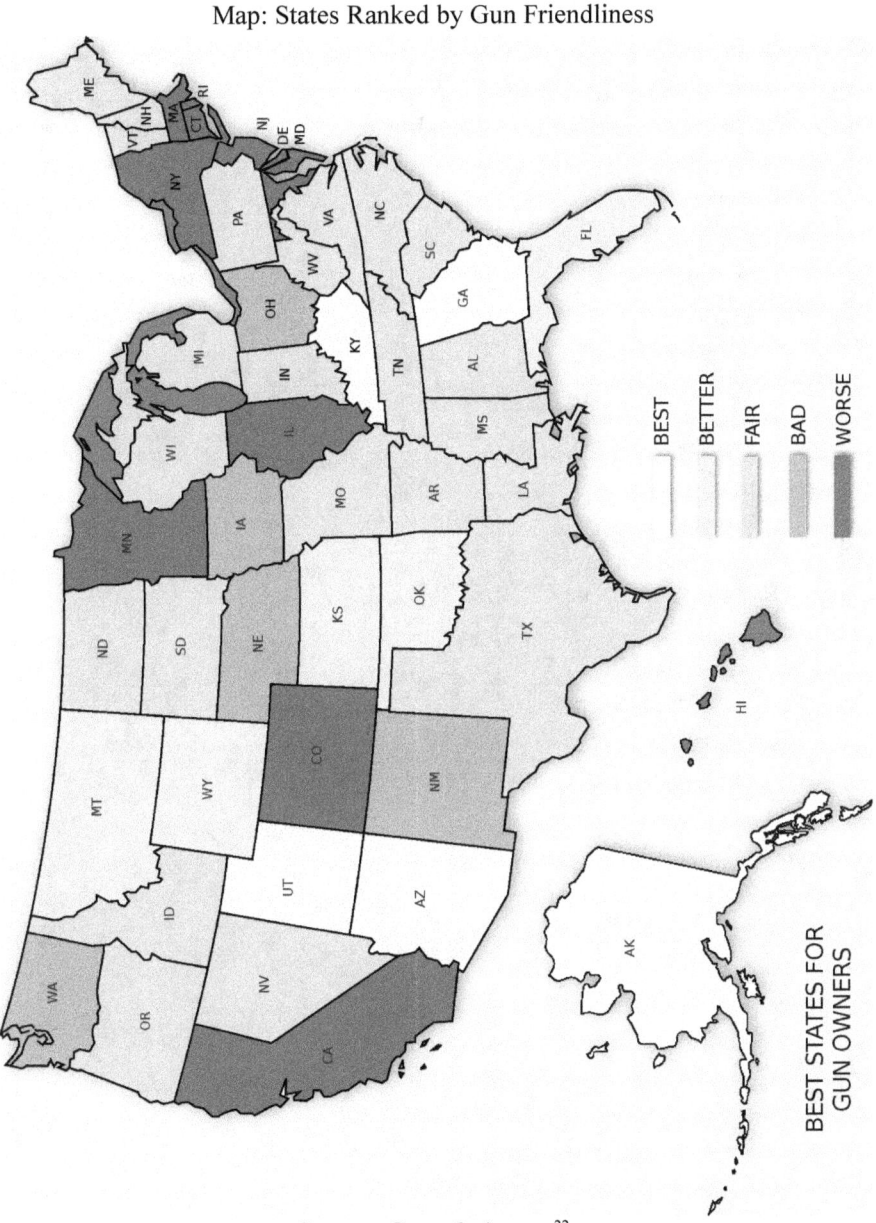

Source: Guns & Ammo[22]

Table: States Ranked by Gun Friendliness

Rank	State	Gun Rank (lower is better)	Score	Rank	State	Gun Rank (lower is better)	Score
1	Arizona	1	200	26	Louisiana	26	100
2	Alaska	2	196	27	Wisconsin	27	96
3	Georgia	3	192	28	Michigan	28	92
4	Utah	4	188	29	Oregon	29	88
5	Kentucky	5	184	30	Idaho	30	84
6	Oklahoma	6	180	31	Pennsylvania	31	80
7	Wyoming	7	176	32	Maine	32	76
8	Montana	8	172	33	Arkansas	33	72
9	Kansas	9	168	34	Nebraska	34	68
10	Florida	10	164	35	New Mexico	35	64
11	Missouri	11	160	36	Ohio	36	60
12	Alabama	12	156	37	Washington	37	56
13	South Dakota	13	152	38	Iowa	38	52
14	Texas	14	148	39	Minnesota	39	48
15	South Carolina	15	144	40	Colorado	40	44
16	Tennessee	16	140	41	Illinois	41	40
17	Vermont	17	136	42	Delaware	42	36
18	Mississippi	18	132	43	Rhode Island	43	32
19	North Carolina	19	128	44	Maryland	44	28
20	North Dakota	20	124	45	Connecticut	45	24
21	Virginia	21	120	46	California	46	20
22	Nevada	22	116	47	Hawaii	47	16
23	West Virginia	23	112	48	Massachusetts	48	12
24	Indiana	24	108	49	New Jersey	49	8
25	New Hampshire	25	104	50	New York	50	4

Source: Guns & Ammo[22]

Crime

The violent crime rate of a state is considered in its suitability as a Bug Out Location or Survival Homestead.

While data for both violent crime and property crime are listed in the tables, only violent crime statistics are used in the maps and to rank the states. The statistics are from the Federal Bureau of Investigation[23].

Table: States Ranked by Crime

Rank	State	Violent crime (per 100k)	Property crime (per 100k)	Score	Rank	State	Violent crime (per 100k)	Property crime (per 100k)	Score
1	Vermont	759	13,875	100	26	Virginia	16,205	170,654	50
2	Wyoming	1,195	12,809	98	27	Colorado	16,226	140,057	48
3	Maine	1,718	30,447	96	28	Nevada	16,824	79,177	46
4	North Dakota	1,954	15,148	94	29	Oklahoma	16,989	126,057	44
5	Montana	2,567	25,953	92	30	Washington	20,153	258,662	42
6	South Dakota	2,674	16,177	90	31	Alabama	20,826	161,993	40
7	Rhode Island	2,705	25,678	88	32	Indiana	23,487	187,536	38
8	New Hampshire	2,849	29,040	86	33	Louisiana	23,984	165,686	36
9	Idaho	3,498	30,055	84	34	South Carolina	24,278	173,049	34
10	Hawaii	3,533	42,875	82	35	New Jersey	25,674	167,556	32
11	Delaware	4,549	28,379	80	36	Missouri	26,197	189,606	30
12	Alaska	4,708	21,210	78	37	Arizona	27,599	225,243	28
13	Nebraska	4,897	49,018	76	38	Massachusetts	27,667	137,285	26
14	West Virginia	5,568	39,013	74	39	Maryland	28,089	157,913	24
15	Utah	6,498	85,586	72	40	Ohio	33,121	338,731	22
16	Mississippi	8,214	81,500	70	41	North Carolina	33,700	308,049	20
17	Iowa	8,388	67,800	68	42	Georgia	36,541	334,399	18
18	Kentucky	9,222	103,857	66	43	Tennessee	38,364	206,629	16
19	Connecticut	9,440	70,990	64	44	Pennsylvania	42,849	263,240	14
20	Kansas	9,838	85,280	62	45	Michigan	44,523	230,334	12
21	Oregon	9,984	124,737	60	46	Illinois	48,974	292,983	10
22	Minnesota	12,705	131,195	58	47	New York	77,372	358,598	8
23	New Mexico	12,782	77,256	56	48	Florida	91,986	607,172	6
24	Arkansas	13,621	106,613	54	49	Texas	107,998	861,734	4
25	Wisconsin	15,961	125,688	52	50	California	154,129	1,018,907	2

Source: Federal Bureau of Investigation[23]

Map: States Ranked by Crime

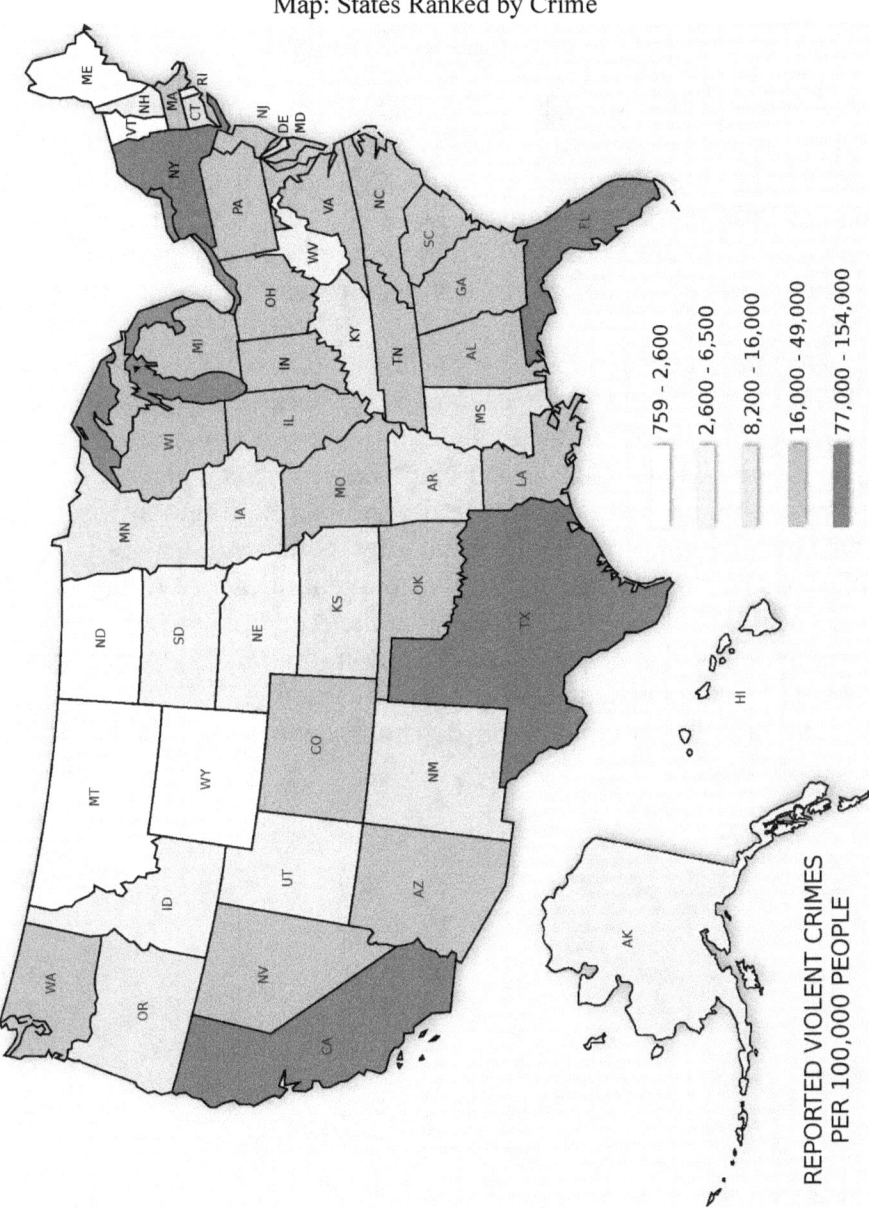

Source: Federal Bureau of Investigation[23]

Population Density

Avoiding proximity to dense population centers is important. Most theories state that in the weeks after a major collapse type event, the city populations will expand outward toward the countryside in search of food. For that reason it is important to choose a Bug Out Location location not only at least 50 miles from a major city, but in an area of few people over a large geographical area.

A state's population density can be further quantified at the county level. Most state or county government web sites can provide such maps showing population density at the county level. The United States Census Bureau[24] has some population density maps with data accurate as of 2012 and can be found at their web site. In addition, ArcGIS manufactures commercial map data but they offer a free online interactive population density map that is very useful. The map can be found at the ArcGIS[25] web site.

Population density weighed heavily in the ranking of the states. The table is quantified in people per square mile.

The source for population densities data is the United States Census Bureau[26].

Map: States Ranked by Population Density

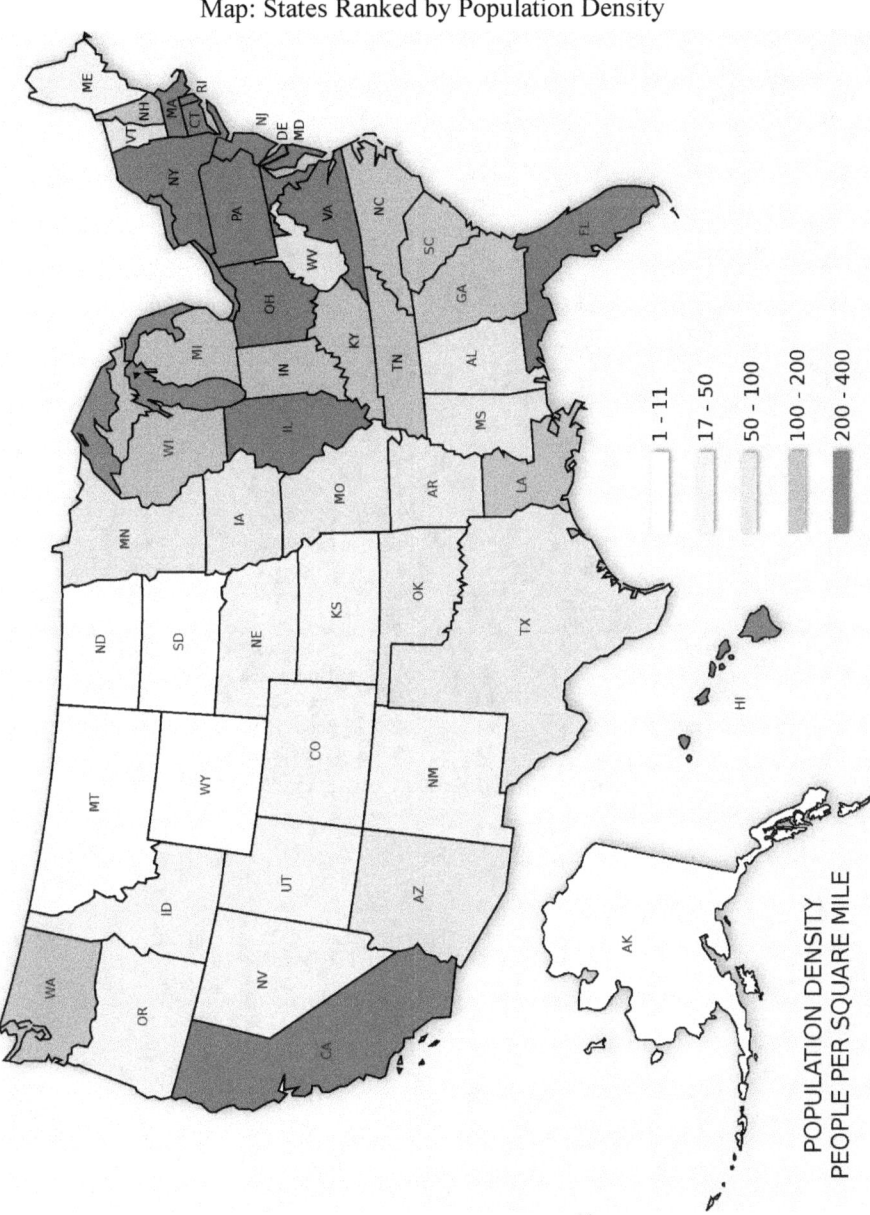

Source: U.S. Census Bureau[26]

Table: States Ranked by Population Density

Rank	State	People per sq mile	Score	Rank	State	People per sq mile	Score
1	Alaska	1.2	150	26	Washington	101.2	75
2	Wyoming	5.8	147	27	Louisiana	104.9	72
3	Montana	6.8	144	28	Wisconsin	105	69
4	North Dakota	9.7	141	29	Kentucky	109.9	66
5	South Dakota	10.7	138	30	New Hampshire	147	63
6	New Mexico	17	135	31	South Carolina	153.9	60
7	Idaho	19	132	31	Tennessee	153.9	60
8	Nebraska	23.8	129	33	Georgia	168.4	54
9	Nevada	24.6	126	34	Michigan	174.8	51
10	Utah	33.6	123	35	Indiana	181	48
11	Kansas	34.9	120	36	North Carolina	196.1	45
12	Oregon	39.9	117	37	Virginia	202.6	42
13	Maine	43.1	114	38	Hawaii	211.8	39
14	Colorado	48.5	111	39	Illinois	231.1	36
15	Iowa	54.5	108	40	California	239.1	33
16	Oklahoma	54.7	105	41	Ohio	282.3	30
17	Arkansas	56	102	42	Pennsylvania	283.9	27
18	Arizona	56.3	99	43	Florida	350.6	24
19	Mississippi	63.2	96	44	New York	411.2	21
20	Minnesota	66.6	93	45	Delaware	460.8	18
21	Vermont	67.9	90	46	Maryland	594.8	15
22	West Virginia	77.1	87	47	Connecticut	738.1	12
23	Missouri	87.1	84	48	Massachusetts	839.4	9
24	Alabama	94.4	81	49	Rhode Island	1018.1	6
25	Texas	96.3	78	50	New Jersey	1195.5	3

Source: United States Census Bureau[26]

Nuclear Power Plants

When searching for a Bug Out Location, most of us will want to find a location sufficiently distant from such a site as to minimize the chance of accumulating radioactive fallout particles in the event of a catastrophic failure of the power plant.

At the time this book is being published, there are 100 commercial nuclear power plants in operation in the continental United States, plus many smaller research facilities spread throughout the country.

The table lists the names and exact locations of all 100 nuclear power plants. The map displayed afterwords gives a visual representation of the locations of the plants, with a graphic representation of the typical prevailing winds. In the event of a catastrophic explosion at a nuclear site (whether by accident or by terrorist attack), radioactive fallout will drift downwind. The optimum Bug Out Location will be located upwind of a nuclear site for this reason.

Keep in mind that a state is not necessarily safe from radioactive fallout because it has no nuclear power plants or research facilities. For example, the state of Maine has no nuclear facilities, but if we examine the map we can see that Maine lies downwind from dozens of nuclear sites.

Nuclear power plants were used in the ranking of the states. The ranking was based on the number of nuclear power plants per square mile. But it may be better to simply use the map when making a final decision in the case of a state like Maine.

Data for nuclear power plants was obtained from the U.S. Nuclear Regulatory Commission[27].

Table: States With Nuclear Power Plants

State	Nuclear Power Reactors in Operation
Alabama	Browns Ferry - Athens, AL (32 miles W of Huntsville, AL) Joseph M. Farley - Columbia, AL (18 miles S of Dothan, AL)
Arizona	Palo Verde - Wintersburg, AZ (50 miles W of Phoenix, AZ)
Arkansas	Arkansas Nuclear - London, AR (6 miles WNW of Russellville, AR)
California	Diablo Canyon Power Plant - Avila Beach, CA (12 miles WSW of San Luis Obispo, CA) Research Reactor: San Ramon, Sunol, Sacremento, Irvine
Colorado	Research Reactor: U.S. Geological Survey - Denver, CO
Connecticut	Millstone Power Station – Waterford, CT (3.2 miles WSW of New London, CT)
Florida	St. Lucie Plant – Jensen Beach, FL (10 miles SE of Ft. Pierce, FL) Turkey Point Nuclear Generating Unit - Homestead, FL (25 miles S of Miami, FL) Research Reactor: University of Florida - Gainesville, FL
Georgia	Edwin I. Hatch - Baxley, GA (20 miles S of Vidalia, GA) Vogtle - Waynesboro, GA (26 miles SE of Augusta, GA)
Idaho	Research Reactor: Idaho State University Pocatello, ID
Illinois	Braidwood - Braceville, IL (20 miles SSW of Joliet, IL) Byron – Byron, IL (17 miles SW of Rockford, IL) Clinton - Clinton, IL (23 miles SSE of Bloomington, IL) Dresden - Morris, IL (23 miles SW of Joliet, IL) La Salle County - Marseilles, IL (11 miles SE of Ottawa, IL) Quad Cities - Cordova, IL (20 miles NE of Moline, IL)
Indiana	Research Reactor: Purdue University West Lafayette, IN
Iowa	Duane Arnold - Palo, IA (8 miles NW of Cedar Rapids, IA)
Kansas	Wolf Creek - Burlington, KS (3.5 miles NE of Burlington, KS) Research Reactor: Kansas State University Manhattan, KS
Louisiana	River Bend - St. Francisville, LA (24 miles NNW of Baton Rouge, LA) Waterford - Killona, LA (25 miles W of New Orleans, LA)
Maryland	Calvert Cliffs - Lusby, MD (40 miles S of Annapolis, MD) Research Reactors: Armed Forces Radiobiology Research Institute Bethesda, MD National Institute of Standards & Technology Gaithersburg, MD University of Maryland College Park, MD
Massachusetts	Pilgrim – Plymouth, MA (38 Miles SE of Boston, MA) Research Reactors: Massachusetts Institute of Technology , Cambridge, MA University of Massachusetts/Lowell , Lowell, MA
Michigan	D.C. Cook - Bridgman, MI (13 miles S of Benton Harbor, MI) Fermi - 25 MI NE of Toledo, OH Palisades - Covert, MI (5 miles S of South Haven, MI) Research Reactor: Dow Chemical Company Midland, MI
Minnesota	Monticello - Monticello, MN (35 miles NW of Minneapolis, MN) Prairie Island - Welch, MN (28 miles SE of Minneapolis, MN)
Mississippi	Grand Gulf - Port Gibson, MS (20 miles SW of Vicksburg, MS)

Source: U.S. Nuclear Regulatory Commission[27]

Table: States With Nuclear Power Plants (continued)

State	Nuclear Power Reactors in Operation
Missouri	Callaway - Fulton, MO (25 miles ENE of Jefferson City, MO) Research Reactors: University of Missouri/Columbia Columbia, MO University of Missouri/Rolla Pool Rolla, MO
Nebraska	Cooper - Brownville, NE (23 miles S of Nebraska City, NE) Fort Calhoun - Ft. Calhoun, NE (19 miles N of Omaha, NE)
New Hampshire	Seabrook - Seabrook, NH (13 miles S of Portsmouth, NH)
New Jersey	Hope Creek - Hancocks Bridge, NJ (18 miles SE of Wilmington, DE) Oyster Creek - Forked River, NJ (9 miles S of Toms River, NJ) Salem - Hancocks Bridge, NJ (18 miles S of Wilmington, DE)
New Mexico	Research Reactor: University of New Mexico Albuquerque, NM
New York	James A. FitzPatrick - Scriba, NY (6 miles NE of Oswego, NY) R.E. Ginna - Ontario, NY (20 miles NE of Rochester, NY) Indian Point - Buchanan, NY (24 miles N of New York City, NY) Nine Mile Point - Scriba, NY (6 miles NE of Oswego, NY) Research Reactor: Rensselaer Polytechnic Institute Troy, NY
North Carolina	Brunswick - Southport, NC (40 miles S of Wilmington, NC) McGuire - Huntersville, NC (17 miles N of Charlotte, NC) Shearon Harris - New Hill, NC (20 miles SW of Raleigh, NC) Research Reactor: North Carolina State University Raleigh, NC
Ohio	Davis-Besse - Oak Harbor, OH (21 miles ESE of Toledo, OH) Perry - Perry, OH (35 miles NE of Cleveland, OH) Research Reactor: Ohio State University Columbus, OH
Oregon	Research Reactors: Oregon State University, Corvallis, OR Reed College
Pennsylvania	Beaver Valley - Shippingport, PA (17 miles W of McCandless, PA) Limerick - Limerick, PA (21 miles NW of Philadelphia, PA) Peach Bottom - Delta, PA (17.9 miles S of Lancaster, PA) Susquehanna - Salem Township, Luzerne County, PA (70 miles NE of Harrisburg, PA) Three Mile Island - Middletown, PA (10 miles SE of Harrisburg, PA) Research Reactor: Pennsylvania State University State College, PA
Rhode Island	Research Reactor: Rhode Island Atomic Energy Commission Narragansett, RI
South Carolina	Catawba - York, SC (18 miles S of Charlotte, NC) Oconee - Seneca, SC (30 miles W of Greenville, SC) H.B. Robinson - Hartsville, SC (26 miles NW of Florence, SC) Virgil C. Summer - Jenkensville, SC (26 miles NW of Columbia, SC)
South Dakota	Pathfinder - Sioux Falls, SD
Tennessee	Sequoyah - Soddy-Daisy, TN (9.5 miles NE of Chattanooga, TN) Watts Bar - Spring City, TN (60 miles SW of Knoxville, TN)

Source: U.S. Nuclear Regulatory Commission[27]

Table: States With Nuclear Power Plants (continued)

State	Nuclear Power Reactors in Operation
Texas	Comanche Peak - Glen Rose, TX (40 miles SW of Fort Worth, TX) South Texas Project - Bay City, TX (90 miles SW of Houston, TX) Research Reactors: Texas A&M University College Station, TX University of Texas Austin, TX
Utah	Research Reactor: University of Utah, Salt Lake City, UT
Vermont	Vermont Yankee - Vernon, VT (5 miles S of Brattleboro, VT)
Virginia	North Anna - Louisa, VA (40 miles NW of Richmond, VA) Surry - Surry, VA (17 miles NW of Newport News, VA)
Washington	Columbia Generating Station - Richland, WA (20 miles NNE of Pasco, WA) Research Reactor: Washington State University Pullman, WA
Wisconsin	Point Beach - Two Rivers, WI (13 miles NNW of Manitowoc, WI) Research Reactor: University of Wisconsin Madison, WI

Source: U.S. Nuclear Regulatory Commission[27]

Map: States With Nuclear Power Plants

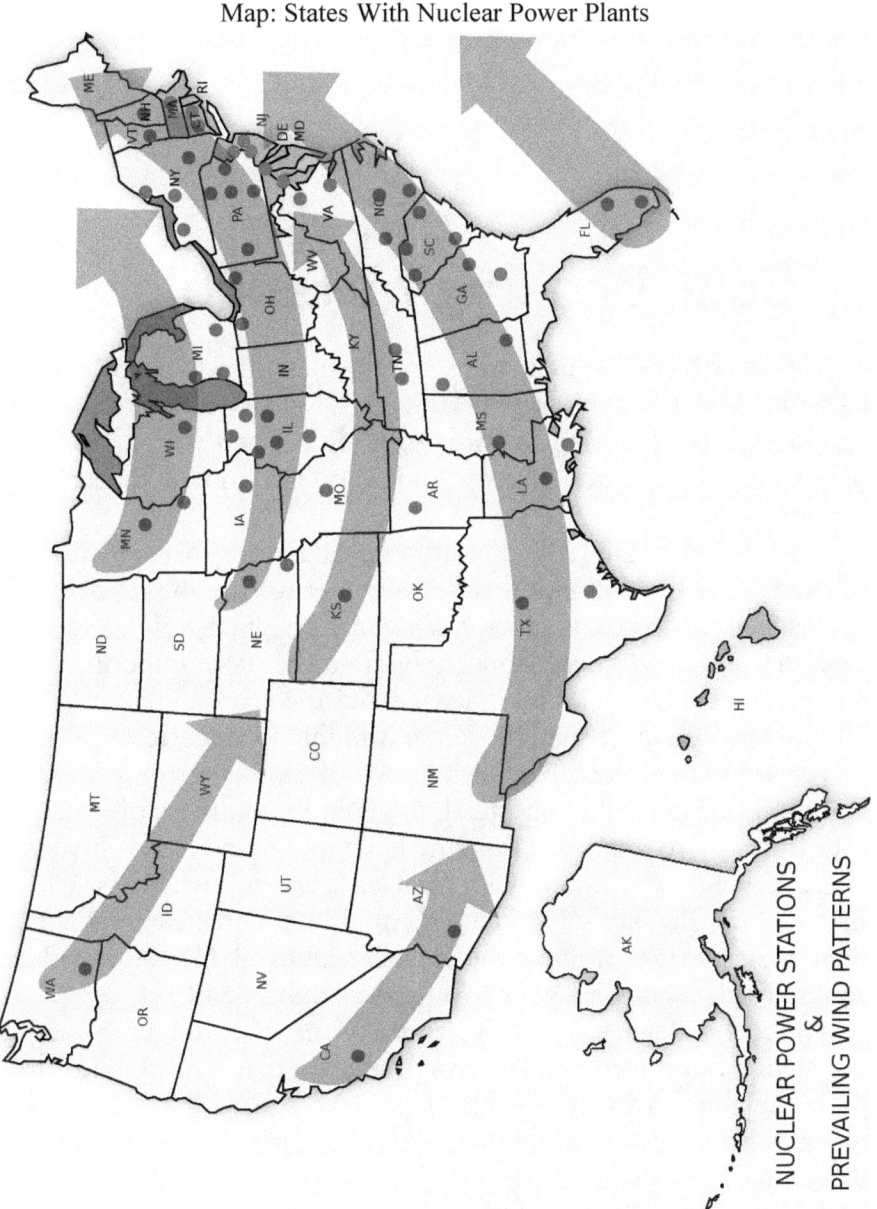

NUCLEAR POWER STATIONS
&
PREVAILING WIND PATTERNS

Source: U.S. Nuclear Regulatory Commission[27]

State Ranking Methodology

The question of which states are the best in which to locate a Bug Out Location or Survival Homestead is subjective, but in the case of this book I tried to come to a logical conclusion based on *only* facts and statistics. The methodology used to rank the states is explained below.

All fifty states are ranked in thirteen categories in a spreadsheet. For the purposes of ranking states together to find the best overall scores, each category is given a *weight*. I assigned weights to each category simply because some categories are more important than others. If a category has a higher weight, the score in that category will be counted more than the lesser-weighted categories.

For example, I decided that in terms of searching for a Bug Out Location or Survival Homestead, the Gun Friendliness of a state is four times more important than the Unemployment Rate. However, not everyone will agree with this assessment, which is why I included *all* the data so people who might not agree can make their own decision. (I will make the spreadsheet available for download so that readers can change the weights as they see fit.)

For each category, I first determined a base score by subtracting the state's rank from 51. This way the state that ranks highest in a given category will get the most points. A state that ranked "1" will have a score of 50, while a state that ranked "50" will have a score of 1.

I then multiplied that score by the weight of the category.

For example, Alabama ranks 14th best in "Per Capita State & Local Tax Burden" and Alaska ranks 6th in that category. In the case of Alabama, subtracting 14 from 51 results in 37. I then multiplied 37 by the category weight of "2" and the result was 74.

So Alabama received a score of 74 in that category, while Alaska, which ranked 6th, received a score of 90:

$$(51 - Rank) \times Weight = Score$$

$$Example: Alabama (51 - 12) \times 2 = 74$$

$$Example: Florida (51 - 6) \times 2 = 90$$

I then simply added up the total scores for each state. The categories and their weights are listed below:

Weight	Category
1	% on Welfare
2	Cost of Living
2	Difference From Median Average temperature
4	Gun Rank
3	People per sq mile
2	Per capita personal income (dollars)
2	Per Capita State & Local Tax Burden
1	Power Plants per 10,000 sq miles
2	Precipitation (inches per year)
1	Unemployment Rate (%)
2	Value of Housing Units (rounded)
2	Violent crime (per 100k)
2	Year Avg. Hours of Solar Potential

Residents on Welfare & Unemployment

These are two categories indicating the economic status of a region. The logic is that the higher percentage of welfare recipients or unemployed workers, the harder it will be to support one's self financially. Although important, these categories are not as important as the other categories in this book and each are assigned a weight of 1.

Per Capita State & Local Tax Burden, Cost of Living, Average Median Income & Value of Housing Units

These categories are also economic in nature, further indicating the financial viability of a state. They will have a more direct bearing on buying property and maintaining a well paying job, so they each have each been assigned a rank of 2.

Violent Crime

The importance of this statistic shouldn't be overlooked. However, it doesn't have a major impact on a state's suitability as a Bug Out Location, so the rate of violent crime per capita is assigned a weight of 2.

Difference From Median Average temperature & Yearly Avg. Hours of Solar Potential

These are two climate related indicators. The Difference From Median Average temperature ranks the states according to how comfortable the temperatures are. This is important because a state with lower temperatures will require heating in the winter and a state with higher temperatures will require cooling in the summer.

The Yearly Average of Solar Potential ranks the states in terms of potential solar electric power. Some states receive greater amounts of sunlight than other states. The relationship between Solar Potential and high temperatures is not linear (you don't always get more sun in the warmer states) so both categories are necessary. Each category is assigned a weight of 2.

Average Annual Precipitation

The tendency of an area to be subject to drought is important when growing crops or harvesting rainwater for drinking. This category was assigned a weight of 2.

Nuclear Power Plants

Most states have at least one nuclear power plant. Odds are that there will never be a problem but the disaster at Fukushima has raised an awareness of the threat.

Nuclear Power Plants was assigned a weight of 1.

Population Density

One of the most important categories, population density, is measured in people per square mile. The lower the population density, the less likely a Bug Out Location or Survival Homestead will be located near a large city. This category is one of the most important and was assigned a weight of 3.

Gun Friendliness

Each state was ranked by Gun Friendliness. Because this category is usually an indicator of the level of personal freedom of a state, and because of the importance of guns to preppers and homesteaders, this category was assigned a weight of 4.

Total State Scores

I was not surprised to see that California, New York, New Jersey, Maryland, Massachusetts, Illinois and Hawaii made up the bottom seven ranking states. Poor guns laws and (in most of those states) high population density combined to make them unsuitable as Survival Homesteads.

I had thought that a few states, like Ohio, Maine, Pennsylvania, Wisconsin, Indiana and Oregon would place higher, but the facts say otherwise.

The top ten ranking states are South Dakota, Wyoming, North Dakota, Kansas, Oklahoma, Utah, Montana, Kentucky, Texas, and Nebraska.

The states with the largest land area scored well. Kansas, Oklahoma, Nebraska and Missouri seem ideal Midwestern states. If the reader must stay east of the Mississippi River, Kentucky or West Virginia would make good choices.

The full spreadsheet is available for viewing on the internet at the author's web site: <https://gordonblaine.wordpress.com/>

Map: States Ranked On All Scores

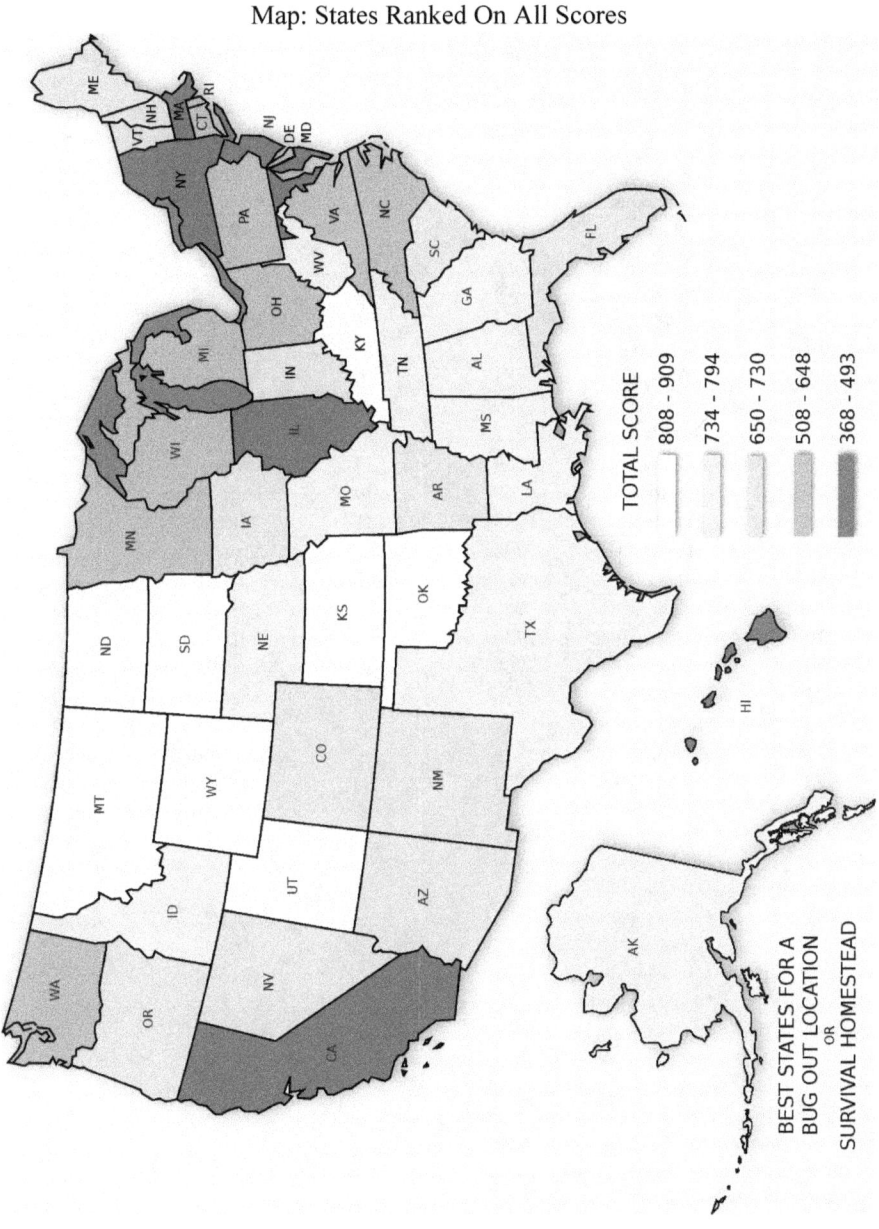

TOTAL SCORE

808 - 909
734 - 794
650 - 730
508 - 648
368 - 493

BEST STATES FOR A
BUG OUT LOCATION
OR
SURVIVAL HOMESTEAD

Table: States Ranked On All Scores

Rank	State	Total Score	Rank	State	Total Score
1	South Dakota	909	26	Vermont	689
2	Wyoming	908	27	Iowa	677
3	North Dakota	903	28	Indiana	673
4	Kansas	902	29	Oregon	659
5	Oklahoma	879	30	South Carolina	657
6	Utah	859	30	Colorado	657
7	Montana	812	32	Maine	650
8	Kentucky	808	33	Washington	648
9	Texas	794	34	North Carolina	629
10	Nebraska	793	35	Virginia	602
11	Alaska	781	36	Wisconsin	575
12	Missouri	780	36	Ohio	575
13	West Virginia	773	38	Delaware	534
14	Idaho	759	39	Pennsylvania	532
15	Louisiana	749	40	Rhode Island	530
16	Tennessee	743	41	Michigan	514
17	Mississippi	741	42	Minnesota	513
18	Alabama	734	43	Connecticut	508
18	Georgia	734	44	Hawaii	493
20	New Hampshire	730	45	Illinois	444
20	Nevada	730	46	Massachusetts	417
22	Arizona	726	47	Maryland	414
23	New Mexico	719	48	New Jersey	384
24	Arkansas	716	49	New York	379
25	Florida	708	50	California	368

Part Four:

How to Research and Buy Real Estate

Searching For Land

The search for the perfect piece of land for your Bug Out Location will require browsing through dozens or hundreds of properties and may take months or years until we find what we need. It can become overwhelming. In one case I personally spent hours researching a property, then I drove an hour to the site and walked around and decided I wanted to buy it. I contacted the seller who told me the property was in the process of being sold to someone else! It was demoralizing and I thought I'd never find what I needed. It takes perseverance and skill to quickly weed out the properties that won't work, then spend our valuable time researching properties that *might* work.

Real Estate Agents

Should you use a real estate agent to help you with your property search?

Certainly, there is no reason *not* to use an agent. If they help you find a property to buy, their fee will be paid by the seller.

Real estate agents have access to resources the rest of us don't. They use special computer software to find properties. They may know of potential properties off the top of their head. Once they find a property (or if you tell them about a property you found) they have the knowledge, skills and experience to find out things about the property and explain them to the buyer. They have personal connections they use to find information on well reports, covenants, and other details of the property that we may have not considered. They set up meetings with sellers, and appointments to see the land.

When I was searching for my Bug Out Location property, I

gave my agent a list of criteria and he went searching. Often I found properties on my own and I would visit him at his office to discuss them. I would say something like, "I wonder if the well on this property is any good?"

My agent said, "I don't know let's find out!"

He called the seller's agent, with whom he already had a working relationship, and within minutes he had a well report and other information in his fax machine. Something that would have taken me hours to accomplish he did with a quick phone call.

After we found a property to purchase, my agent handled the negotiating with the seller to settle upon a price and he looked out for our best interests, ensuring the proper paperwork was done to protect us. He even set up the title search with the title company (I was paying cash for the property, so technically I wasn't required to do the title search).

It was a very satisfying experience. And I must add, although I spent many hours searching for property on my own, it was my agent who found the property I ultimately bought.

Internet Searches

The great thing about searching for land on the internet is that there is (compared to newspapers) a lot of information about each property visible at a glance in each listing. Usually there is at least one picture and an address, driving directions, or GPS coordinates, and sometimes a USGS map. When looking at off grid properties, the listing usually says if the property is accessible year-round. If there is a well, it will be listed, along with creeks, ponds or springs.

Newspapers and Circular Advertisements

At one time, newspapers were the only way of searching for property. They are still worth investigating, but often there is too little information posted in the ads. The charge to place newspaper classified ad is usually determined by how many lines of text are in the ad, so they are kept as small as possible. Often each ad is just a few lines of text and they may not even include the size of the acreage and occasionally they don't mention the price of the land!

Circular ads are usually more informative, but they tend to highlight the properties that will make the most money for the distributor and in my experience usually don't have bare land at a reasonable cost.

For these reasons I had much better luck using a real estate agent and the internet. But they are worth checking every now and then.

Check The Land

After you have found a piece of property that may be suitable, spend a few hours researching it.

When searching for my Bug Out Location property, I found that much work can be done on the internet and many properties can be ruled out before spending time traveling or dealing with sellers or real estate agents.

Whether the land was found on the internet, through the newspapers, or with an agent, if the address or GPS coordinates are available the property may be found on Google Maps. Satellite imagery can give detailed and fairly up-to-date information. Roads, trees, bodies of water, and buildings can usually be seen on these images, giving a good idea of the layout of the land and the proximity of neighbors.

With Google Earth, a 3D view of the land can be overlaid with the satellite imagery. The user can zoom down to ground level and pan around to see if mountains will obstruct the southern sky, which can be very useful to see if gardens will grow or solar power is feasible.

Another option for checking the terrain on a map is to find the property on a USGS terrain map[28], the kind hikers and backpackers use.

Most states or counties have web sites allowing property to be researched on line. The state in which my Bug Out Location is located has an excellent web site called Montana Cadastral[29], with an interactive map. The map can be zoomed in to individual parcels where details can be seen such as the owner name, zoning, property size, and taxes.

Once the internet work has been done and a property is found meeting the requirements, it is time to visit the site in person. Walk the land, preferably with a knowledgeable real estate agent or with the owner, and check the following:

- Find the corner posts marking the boundaries. If they are unable to be located, a surveying company may need to be hired. If the buyer is comfortable with the approximate boundaries, the survey may be contracted by the seller upon agreement of the sale. Note that fencing may not be actually on the property boundary.

- Look for signs of pollution or contamination, or signs of recreational use. If the land has been used by recreational users (or drug users) for years, they may be a problem for the new land owner.

- See if your cell phone has a connection, even a very weak one. There are free apps that will indicate if there is a signal too weak to show any bars. If there is any kind of signal at all, it can be made usable with a cell phone repeater.

- Check the view to the south to make sure it is clear for gardening, solar power, or satellite TV connection. There are cell phone apps you can use to locate TV satellites. Tall trees on the property can be cleared, but hills or trees on a property to the south may be a problem.

- Inspect any timber to determine the species and quantity of wood.

- See if the soil is good for growing. Dig a small hole and check for the presence of organic matter or an abundance of clay or sand. Look for rocks on the surface, which may indicate even more rocks below the ground, making gardening and fencing difficult. Look for obnoxious invasive weeds. A property overrun with knapweed or kudzu might be a problem.

- Look for surface water or evidence of a potential spring. An undeveloped spring may show as a wet spot or seep on the side of a hill. In my area aspen trees like to grow in moist soil; look for trees or bushes that like water. If you find a spring, don't let the seller know! He may use it as a negotiating point.

Note that if the land has surface water or wetlands, the EPA may restrict what can be done with the property. The buyer may have to notify them and pay for an expensive study before they will allow a residence (or any other building) to be built on the property.

Assuming the internet search for more information was a dead end, some old fashioned footwork can be performed. Public records should be available at the local county which can determine the seller's name and the taxable value of the property, as well as taxes paid and whether tax payments have been made.

At the county office the zoning of the property can be determined. Maps may be available to determine if the property has access roads.

If the property has a well, the well record should be obtained. This will detail the depth of the well and the refill rate.

At the county office where my Bug Out Location is located, I was able to chat with a helpful employee about the property. He was friendly and full of information. He even told me that based on his memory of the area, he thought it should pass a "perk test", allowing a septic system. I also got a good idea of the process of getting a septic system permitted and he gave me the name of a local company to do the work.

Zoning

When considering a piece of land for purchase, consider the zoning of the property. All land is subject to zoning by the local government to determine what is allowed be done on the land. The idea is to keep commercial areas separated from residential areas, so Commercial zoning and Residential zoning are the most common zones.

In terms of a Bug Out Location, there are other zoning types we should consider.

Agricultural zones are appealing because they limit the density of development. If an area is zoned Agricultural, the chances of a housing subdivision popping up next to your Bug Out Location are unlikely. Of course an influential developer may convince the local government to change the zoning of the area, so it is not a sure-fire guarantee.

Rural zoning is set for farms or ranches but in some cases will include residences to allow horses or cattle.

In addition, tax rates are lower in Agricultural and Rural zones.

Watch out for Recreational zoning! Some Recreational zoned property can not legally be lived at year-round.

Title Search

Before granting a mortgage loan, the bank may require a Title Search. In any case, I recommend that *the agreement to purchase a property* be contingent upon acceptable results of a title search. A title search consists of reviewing historical documents relevant to the property and is usually hired out to a title company or escrow agent at a cost of $100-$500, but the search may be performed by the buyer because most of the required documents are a matter of public record. My personal feeling is to let the experts do it.

The title search will reveal, among other things, the chain of title. Every person or entity who ever owned the property will be in the chain of title. This can be interesting. For example, the title search for my Bug Out Location property revealed that the first listed owner was the railroad company, who had been granted the land by the US government in the 1800's to build the railroad.

The results of the title search will determine a few other important things, some of which may be completely unknown to the seller.

Is the seller the actual owner of the property and able to sell it?

As unbelievable as it sounds, there are con men out there selling property they don't own. In other cases, the seller may honestly believe they own the property and are able sell it, but for one legal reason or another they are unable to do so. It may be a matter where a distant relative, completely unknown to the seller, has a legal claim to the property. Years after you purchase the property, the distant relative may come forward to claim the property and put you in a difficult legal and financial bind.

Are there liens on the property?

These may include tax liens and mortgages and will complicate the purchase of the property, and they may be unknown to the seller. These obstacles can be overcome, but it is better to find out about them before a purchase agreement is made.

Are there restrictions on the property?

Restrictions may be easements or covenants. Easements grant another party access to the property. It may be that the utility company has a right-of-way to access electrical poles, or you may have a road on the property that a neighbor uses to access his property. In my opinion these may be of little consequence; I have an easement road on my property that my neighbor uses to get to his house and I use easement roads to get to my own property. However, easements should be considered and the buyer should make the decision whether or not they are acceptable.

Covenants limit what the buyer can do with the property. The purchaser of land for use as a Bug Out Location should think twice about land that comes with such restrictions. We may think we can live with them now, but what if we change our mind later? For example, when I was searching for land for my Bug Out Location I looked at properties that had restrictions stating that no swine may be raised on the property. Otherwise these properties were perfect. I had no plans to raise pigs at the time so it didn't seem to be a big deal. I went with my gut feeling and decided not to make an offer. Later, when I began researching farming methods in greater detail, I realized I had made the right decision.

Water, mineral, and timber rights

Make sure the property comes with the water, mineral and timber rights. In terms of water rights, the buyer may not legally be able to use the water that comes with the property; even water below the ground.

Mineral and timber rights may be granted to outside parties to access your land. Imagine visiting your land to find out the natural gas company has cleared most of the trees and is drilling for gas! Or that the local logging company has clear-cut all your timber. If those companies own the mineral or timber rights for your property they can do this legally and there isn't a thing you can do about it. The person who sold you the property may not have known about the loss of timber or mineral rights because it may have been his great-great-grandfather who sold them!

Buying Real Estate

Purchasing real estate can be a complicated process with details beyond the understanding of mere mortals and it is best to have the assistance of at least one expert. When paying cash for property, the real estate agent and the organization providing the title search may be all the assistance required, providing you do your own due diligence. When paying with a mortgage loan, it is best to have a real estate attorney in your corner to look out for your best interests.

This book is focused on *finding* Bug Out Property. To describe all the details of purchasing real estate should be a book of its own, but I will describe a few basic concepts below.

Mortgage Loans

Unless we have plenty of cash saved up (or we have assets we can sell to get money) we are probably going to have to take out a loan to buy our property.

Most real estate is purchased with a mortgage loan because it allows a person to buy the property without having to pay the entire amount up front. Detailing a mortgage loan is the subject for a book of it's own, but I will outline some of the major points.

Mortgage loan is a loan secured by property. This means if the borrower fails to meet the terms of the loan (make the payments on time and for the duration of the terms) the lender can seize the property.

Most real estate loans are set for 10 years, 15, years, 20 years and 30 years. The longer the loan terms, the smaller the monthly payments. But total interest paid on the longer term loans will be higher.

Mortgage loans can have a fixed interest rate, an adjustable interest rate (ARM), or a combination of the two. Obviously, with a fixed interest rate loan, the interest rate remains fixed over the life of the loan. An ARM may have a fixed interest rate for the first payments, but then the interest rate may fluctuate based on movements on an interest rate index. ARMs are for more experienced borrowers.

Mortgage loans usually require a down payment, sometimes up to 20% of the value of the property.

Mortgaged loan payments consist of interest and principal, and may include taxes and insurance. The earlier loan payments may consist of very little principal and may be almost entirely interest. As the loan payments progress throughout the term, the ratio shifts toward more payment on principal and less on interest.

Not only financial institutions lend money in the form of a mortgage loan. Sometimes sellers of real estate (especially in remote areas) will provide their own loan. These loans are just as binding as bank loans, but the lender may or may not require a credit check.

The interest on a mortgage loan can end up being a large part of the total cost of the property. There are many mortgage loan calculators on the internet and it is worthwhile to plug in some numbers and get an idea of monthly payments and total cost of the mortgage.

For example, let's say we found a piece of property that we like and the selling price is $100,000. We have enough cash for a 10% down payment, which would set the mortgage loan amount at $90,000. The bank will give you the loan with an interest rate of 3.8%.

With a 30 year mortgage our monthly payments (not including taxes and insurance) would be $419. At the end of the loan we would have paid a total of $150,970. We would end up paying almost $61,000 to borrow $90,000!

But if we change the terms of the loan to a ten year payback period, the payments will increase to $903, over twice as much as our 30-year loan. Total payments at the end of the ten years would be $108,321, saving us $42,649 and costing us $18,321 to borrow that same $90,000.

Agent Fees & Closing Costs

If real estate agents are used in the transaction they will need to get paid for their work. The good news when buying property is that the agents are paid by the seller, which means that there is no reason to not use a real estate agent to purchase land!

Closing costs are a different matter. The bulk of closing costs are bank fees, so they will only apply if you are borrowing money from the bank to buy the property. They are usually made up of fees for document preparation, escrow for taxes, wiring fees and insurance and recording fees, and title search fees. They usually total up to about 3.5% of the value of the loan. On a $100,000 loan that adds up to $3,500, which is a substantial chunk of money.

Closing costs are usually paid by the buyer, but negotiations can be made where they are paid by the seller.

How To Own Land Anonymously

Earlier I discussed how easy it is to find information on properties on the internet or by visiting the county office directly. This is a double edged sword; once we own property it is just as easy for other people to find information about it and about us.

But it is possible, for reasons of privacy, to purchase or own property without directly using your name. There are various justifications for doing so. Celebrities do it all the time so people can't find out where they live. Another reason may be to avoid frivolous lawsuits; if someone can find your net worth, they may be more inclined to sue you. If your name is not listed as the owner you will not show up in a casual search of the county records.

There are two common ways to own property without using your name; LLCs and trusts. There are a couple things I should mention; purchasing land anonymously may be difficult if you are financing a mortgage, and whichever method is used, you are still linked to the property. Although you will have some protection from the casual seeker, a determined individual will find you. And there is no hiding from the government!

LLC

In this case, the property is purchased in the name of a Limited Liability Corporation (LLC). Forming an LLC is simple; choose a business name meeting the state's requirements and file the paperwork with the state. Filing fees vary depending on the state. In my state (Montana) the filing fee is $70 and the process is completed within 10 business days.

One benefit of buying property with an LLC is that they limit personal vulnerability to potential lawsuits related to the property. If someone sues you because of damages incurred on your property, they sue the LLC for damages and not you personally.

Trusts

Another way to own property anonymously is by using a title holding trust. The parts making up a trust are the trust agreement, the trustee, and the beneficiary. The trustee is the person who's name is listed on the title and he or she signs all official documents. The trustee can be anyone, including an attorney. The Beneficiary is the person who uses the land.

Part Five:

You Have Your Property - Now What?

What To Do Now?

After you have obtained the property for your Bug Out Location and made preparations to visit (whether during a crisis or not), it is time to make a priority list of things to improve or to develop from scratch:

1. Water source
2. Dwelling (shelter)
3. Food

These are the Big Three. I put food at the bottom of the list because if you need to bug out immediately you can bring a supply of food with you. You can also bring in water, but we need more water than food and water is heavier and harder to transport. If we have a source of water on the property it will make the situation much more survivable.

Shelter is next in importance not only because we don't want to die of exposure, but a good shelter is essential to improving morale and boosting the will to live.

Also, of lesser immediate importance are a means to cook meals, keep warm (if needed), a way to light the dwelling at night and a way to keep the family busy or entertained during the sudden and stressful turn of events. I know from experience that taking the teenagers to the family Bug Out Location even for recreational purposes can lead to tension in the family conversations.

When thinking about the long term survivability of the Bug Out Location, I found that these items should have priority after the Big Three:

1. Establish a survival garden
2. Fencing to keep animals out of the gardens (including the two-legged animals)
3. Water piping infrastructure for irrigating gardens
4. Fencing to contain livestock
5. Water piping infrastructure for the livestock
6. Shelters for livestock
7. Provide an independent source of electrical power (solar, wind, hydro, generator)
8. Establish the woodlot

Future books in the Survival Homestead series will focus on development of those items.

Author's Note

Find full size maps, tables and links to other related information
at the author's web site:
https://gordonblaine.wordpress.com/

If you enjoyed this book, please be kind enough to leave a
review at:
http://www.amazon.com/dp/B00UW9SOTS

Other books by Gordon Blaine:

Montana Homestead: How I Built My Bugout Homestead Off
Grid In The Wilderness
http://www.amazon.com/dp/B00S1SNL90

Charlie's Burden: A Short Story
http://www.amazon.com/dp/B00TMICM0C

Coming Soon:
Survival Homestead Two: Designing the Survival Homestead
Survival Homestead Three: Survival Gardening
Survival Homestead Four: Solar Power At The Homestead
Survival Homestead Five: The Timber Lot

Acknowledgments

Thanks to my wife for helping me with this book and for putting up with me in general, and to my daughter for providing artistic help with the cover design.

Thanks to my friends at the forum for beta reading and providing valuable insight and opinions:

6.8SPC , Fillzee, Preacherboy, JimET, johnmcd, BaldDad, HB of CJ, Aubb, Metcalf, Dragonid, BmassBMore, Harry The Cat, tblount, East Coast Woods, shado, Goodwrench708, txprep, Nomad-max, Sarkus, marketermac, Shadowstalker, HorseSoldier, kmon, CaveIn, 9111315, MikeK, CCW, Sulfur, ajole, superflux, ecocks, ForestBeekeeper, and warmpod

About the Author

A descendant of the Amish, Gordon Blaine's life is a juxtaposition of primitive yearnings and cutting edge tech. He spends his time improving his Bug Out Location in the remote Montana wilderness where he spends his days making lumber on his sawmill, editing LISP code, feeding the livestock and trying to whittle down a perpetually growing honey-do list.

Endnotes

1. Blaine, Gordon. *Montana Homestead: How I Built My Homestead Off Grid In The Wilderness*. N.p.: Sarco Press, 13 Jan. 2015. Web. <http://www.amazon.com/dp/B00S1SNL90>.

2. Christian, Eric R. "Coronal Mass Ejections." *NASA's Cosmicopia*. NASA.gov, 5 Mar. 2012. Web. 10 Feb. 2015. <http://helios.gsfc.nasa.gov/cme.html>.

3. "USDA Plant Hardiness Zone Map." *USDA Plant Hardiness Zone Map*. United States Department of Agriculture, n.d. Web. <http://www.planthardiness.ars.usda.gov>.

4. "NOAA's National Climatic Data Center (NCDC)." National Climatic Data Center (NCDC). N.p., n.d. Web. 18 Mar. 2015. <http://www.ncdc.noaa.gov>.

5. "Climate Prediction Center - Monitoring & Data: Degree Days Statistics."*Climate Prediction Center - Monitoring & Data: Degree Days Statistics*. National Weather Service, n.d. Web. 10 Feb. 2015.
<http://www.cpc.ncep.noaa.gov/products/analysis_monitoring/cdus/degree_days>.

6. "Degree Days.net - Custom Degree Day Data." *Heating & Cooling Degree Days*. BizEE Software Limited, n.d. Web. 10 Feb. 2015. <http://www.degreedays.net>.

7. "Ashburn, VA." *Weather Forecast & Reports*. The Weather Channel, LLC, n.d. Web. 10 Feb. 2015. <http://www.wunderground.com>.

8. "BTU Calculator." *BTU Calculator*. Maple Tech, n.d. Web. 10 Feb. 2015. <http://www.calculator.net/btu-calculator.html>.

9. "Annual Heating Degree Days." Annual Heating Degree Days. National Climatic Data Center, n.d. Web. 10 Feb. 2015. <http://www.ncdc.noaa.gov/img/documentlibrary/clim81supp3/annualheatingDD_hires.jpg>

10. "Annual Cooling Degree Days." Annual Cooling Degree Days. National Climatic Data Center, n.d. Web. 10 Feb. 2015. <http://www.ncdc.noaa.gov/img/documentlibrary/clim81supp3/annualcoolingDD_hires.jpg>

11. "Historical Palmer Drought Indices." *Historical Palmer*

Drought Indices. National Climatic Data Center (NCDC), n.d. Web. 09 Feb. 2015. <http://www.ncdc.noaa.gov/temp-and-precip/drought/historical-palmers/>.

12. "Solar Maps." *NREL: Dynamic Maps, GIS Data, and Analysis Tools*. National Renewable Energy Laboratory, n.d. Web. 10 Feb. 2015. <http://www.nrel.gov/gis/solar.html>.

13. "Residential-Scale 30-Meter Wind Maps." *WINDExchange:*. U.S. Department of Energy, n.d. Web. 10 Feb. 2015. <http://apps2.eere.energy.gov/wind/windexchange/windmaps/residential_scale.asp>.

14. "Wind Maps." *NREL: Dynamic Maps, GIS Data, and Analysis Tools*. National Renewable Energy Laboratory, n.d. Web. 10 Feb. 2015. <http://www.nrel.gov/gis/wind.html>.

15. "ArcGIS Woods Hole US Biomass" *Woods Hole US Biomass*. ESRI, n.d. Web. 10 Feb. 2015. <http://www.arcgis.com/home/webmap/viewer.html?webmap=f7535ebbb05b4eaf8ef019dbeb42be19>.

16. "Biomass Maps." *NREL: Dynamic Maps, GIS Data, and Analysis Tools*. National Renewable Energy Laboratory, n.d. Web. 10 Feb. 2015. <http://www.nrel.gov/gis/biomass.html>.

17. "NASA Visible Earth: Where the Trees Are." *NASA Visible Earth: Where the Trees Are*. NASA, n.d. Web. 10 Feb. 2015. <http://visibleearth.nasa.gov/view.php?id=76697>.

18. "Regional Data." *U.S. Bureau of Economic Analysis (BEA)*. U.S. Department of Commerce, n.d. Web. 7 Feb. 2015. <http://bea.gov/regional/index.htm>. (2013 data)

19. Elise Gould, Nicholas Finio, Natalie Sabadish, and Hilary Wething. "Family Budget Calculator." *Economic Policy Institute*. N.p., n.d. Web. 27 Feb. 2015. <http://www.epi.org/resources/budget>.

20. "Unemployment Rates for States." *U.S. Bureau of Labor Statistics*. U.S. Bureau of Labor Statistics, n.d. Web. 10 Feb. 2015. <http://www.bls.gov/web/laus/laumstrk.htm>. (2014 data)

21. U.S. Department of Commerce. U.S. Census Bureau | American FactFinder. *Median Housing Value of Owner-Occupied Housing Units (Dollars) - State -- County / County Equivalent*. Web. 7 Feb. 2015. <http://factfinder.census.gov/faces/tableservices/jsf/pages/productv

iew.xhtml?pid=ACS_09_5YR_GCT2510.ST05&prodType=table>
(2009 data)

22. "Best States for Gun Owners 2014 - Guns & Ammo." *Guns Ammo Best States for Gun Owners 2014 Comments*. N.p., n.d. Web. 06 Feb. 2015. <http://www.gunsandammo.com/network-topics/culture-politics-network/best-states-for-gun-owners-2014/>.

23. "Offenses Known to Law Enforcement." *Uniform Crime Reports*. Federal Bureau of Investigation, Sept. 2014. Web. 22 Feb. 2015. <http://www.fbi.gov/about-us/cjis/ucr/crime-in-the-u.s/2013/crime-in-the-u.s.-2013/offenses-known-to-law-enforcement/offenses-known-to-law-enforcement>. (2013 data)

24. "United States Census Bureau." *Thematic Maps*. United States Census Bureau, n.d. Web. 10 Feb. 2015. <https://www.census.gov/geo/maps-data/maps/thematic.html>.

25. *USA Population Density*. Esri, n.d. Web. 10 Feb. 2015. <http://www.arcgis.com/home/item.html?id=302d4e6025ef41fa8d3525b7fc31963a>.

26. R. "U.S. Census Bureau, Statistical Abstract of the United States: 2012." *Table 14. State Population—Rank, Percent Change, and Population Density: 1980 to 2010* (n.d.): n. pag. Web.

27. "Nuclear Reactors." *NRC: Nuclear Reactors*. U.S. Nuclear Regulatory Commission, n.d. Web. 10 Feb. 2015. <http://www.nrc.gov/reactors.html>.

28. *US Geological Survey Maps*, http://www.usgs.gov/

29. *Montana Cadastral*, http://svc.mt.gov/msl/mtcadastral/